One True Scrapper

A Memoir of Childhood Cancer,
Good Eyeliner,
and a Fighting Spirit

Kaden Peebles

Library of Congress Cataloging-in-Publication Data

Names: Peebles, Kaden, author.
Title: One true scrapper : a memoir of teen cancer, good eyeliner, and a
    fighting spirit / Kaden Peebles.
Identifiers: LCCN 2023020968 | ISBN 9781944528225 (paperback)
Subjects: LCSH: Peebles, Kaden--Health. | Ewing's
    sarcoma--Patients--Arkansas--Biography. |
    Leukemia--Patients--Arkansas--Biography. | Young
    women--Arkansas--Biography. | Arkansas--Biography.
    BISAC: BIOGRAPHY & AUTOBIOGRAPHY / Personal Memoirs |
    BIOGRAPHY & AUTOBIOGRAPHY / Medical (incl. Patients) |
    HEALTH & FITNESS /Diseases & Conditions / Cancer
Classification: LCC RC280.B6 P44 2023 | DDC 362.1/969947160092
    [B]--dc23/eng/20230601
LC record available at https://lccn.loc.gov/2023020968

Et Alia Press titles are available at special discounts when purchased in
quantity directly from the Press. For details,
contact hello@etaliapress.com or the address below.

Published in the United States of America by:
Et Alia Press
PO Box 7948
Little Rock, AR 72217
hello@etaliapress.com
etaliapress.com

In loving memory of Andrew:

The sunshine in my life and the fire in my soul.

"I'll love you forever, I'll like you for always. As long as I'm living, my baby you'll be." — Robert Munsch

In honor of PaPaw:

Thank you for making all of my dreams possible. Everything I am, and know, and do, is because of you.

Part 1

1

I woke early to the bustling noises of nurses reporting to each other, doctors gathering in preparation to round, and IV pumps beeping down the halls—all signs of shift change.

Groggily, I rolled out of the hospital bed and dragged my IV pole behind me. As I entered the bathroom, I saw my reflection in the mirror. A spot on my head where the hair was missing caught my eye. With only the gentle pull of my fingers, the silky locks that had brushed my shoulders the day before now fell out in clumps.

Gasping, I turned toward the doorway where Mother stood. She stepped over the threshold and squeezed me tightly as hot tears brimmed at the edges of my eyelids. I held in a breath, almost as if holding it could contain my sorrow, almost as if holding it in could stop time.

This new bald spot made everything real. Without my hair, who was I?

Mother let go of me, patting me on the shoulder with reassurance.

I stepped back toward the bed where I'd been spending countless hours. It was too much. I needed to sit down.

As I sat at the edge of my bed, Mother whispered, "Kaden . . ." My eyes went to her and then followed her line of vision to my pillow, where strands of my long dark hair stood out harshly against the white pillowcase.

I thought, *This is it. Here it goes. This is really happening.*

While I was warned by doctors and nurses that my hair would fall out due to the powerful chemotherapies, part of me believed it would not really happen to me. I would be the rare case. If I stopped using flat irons and blow dryers, I figured it might even keep growing. My thick hair had always grown well. Since I had intentionally fixed my hair every day in appreciation, since it was important to me, it would stay.

But there was so much hair that morning. While I still had quite a bit on my head, it was falling out effortlessly, and it was everywhere.

Mother offered to cut my hair from mid-back to chin length. She suggested that the lighter weight might keep some of it intact so that Maddi could shave it when I got home the following week. I thought back to a promise I'd made to Maddi, one of my best friends since we were little girls, that she could be the one to shave my head if my hair began falling out after chemo. It never occurred to me that it might start falling out before I'd even left the hospital.

I didn't want it to be short, but I was losing it all anyway, so I relented. Mother crawled in bed with me and began cutting with a pair of craft scissors. Despite my head feeling lighter, an invisible weight pressed down on my shoulders. She cut, and we both cried as my hair fell away.

Little did I know that this was just the start to years that only God, chemo, and good eyeliner would get me through.

From the day I was born, others have described me as sassy and bold. People have typically either loved or hated my extra-ness, and from the haters, I've gotten the drift that my fierce, energetic personality is a flaw.

As a child, I often felt ashamed, because I didn't understand why I'd find myself "in trouble" when I hadn't actually broken any rules. In elementary school, a teacher told my parents that I had good grades, never disobeyed her in class, and always used my manners, but that I was "too flamboyant." When my parents relayed the news from the not-so-positive parent-teacher conference, I struggled to grasp the meaning. As a little girl raised to always use my best manners and follow the rules, I was unaware of the difference between breaking rules and just being too overwhelming for adults with authority.

Over the years, teachers, coaches, and other adults in

my life gave my parents the same account using different adjectives. They would say I had too much energy or was too loud or asked too many questions—all the emphasis on *too*. For a long time, I thought something was wrong with me. Was my personality built wrong for this world? I struggled for years, but despite being told in so many ways that I was "too much," my spirit remained bold.

In some ways, my boldness was an asset. During the summer between fifth and sixth grades, I began tumbling lessons at a gym that had teams in All Star Cheer competitions. One of the coaches saw potential in my weak round-offs and recruited me to join an All Star Cheer team. As the youngest member at age 11, I had much room to improve compared to girls in their senior year of high school. But the love of performing the routines with my teammates motivated me to better my skills. Over time, my jumps got higher, my dance moves sharpened, and I learned more. The better my skills became, the more I enjoyed performing and competing. I had transitioned from competing in pageants for the first nine years of my life to competing on the mat, and cheerleading soon took the place that pageants had once held. Both hobbies gave me the opportunity to be on the stage and perform.

In junior high, I decided to try out for the cheer squad. I had my back handspring down, stretched daily to improve my jumps, and worked to perfect the required cheers and dances for tryouts. Confidence was not an issue. I believed in myself, and because of my experience with my competitive cheer squad, I truly believed I would make seventh-grade cheerleader.

When the day of tryouts arrived, I felt great. I nailed my tryout and had no doubt I would make the team. Later, I sat crisscross in the living room next to Mother as we listened to the local radio station for the results to be announced. After waiting about an hour, I heard the school district athletic director's voice come over the speakers.

"Just remember," Mother said to me softly, "even if you don't make the team, everything will still be okay." I heard her but felt certain it wasn't going to be an issue.

As the athletic director announced the girls who made the squad, more and more names were going by, and he had not yet said "Kaden Peebles." My anxiety grew, and my heart pumped fast.

He came to the end of the list. I began to cry, and Mother quickly scooped me up in her arms and attempted to console my broken heart. *What did I do wrong?*

"I knew there was a chance I wouldn't make it, but I didn't really think it would happen to me!" I exclaimed to Mother, nearly breathless.

We went on to discuss the odds as the reality set in that I would not spend my seventh-grade year on my school cheer squad. Luckily, I still had my competitive cheer team, but the disappointment persisted.

Over the next year, I spent many nights in the gym taking tumbling lessons, conditioning my body, and practicing routines. I worked hard and won several national titles with my competitive cheer squad. When tryout time rolled around again, I decided to give it another shot. This time, I went into tryouts understanding that there was a possibility I wouldn't make the team, but still feeling confident and believing failure would not actually happen again. Despite having another good tryout, the results were the same. I was almost more shocked to not make the team the second time. I had worked extremely hard, and my competitive cheer coaches had built up my faith in my skills once again, only for it to be shattered.

When it was time for ninth-grade tryouts, I was done. I had been burned too many times. I was no longer cheering with my competitive squad and was not planning on trying out for my school squad. When tryout sign-ups came out, I held off.

But there was a particular sixth grader who signed up to try out for her seventh-grade year: my sister, Breanna. She was tall and flexible, making her a good back spot and high jumper.

Breanna had watched me try out and not make the team for two years, but she had also watched me earn many wins with my competitive cheer squad. Mother and Bre worked together to encourage me to try out once again. At first I was adamant, but once they finally broke through my stubborn walls, they were able to remind me of my love for the sport. I decided that it would be gratifying to cheer with my sister since we had always done everything else together. So, I put past disappointment behind me, and for the third time, tried out for my junior high cheer squad. We both made it! We were ecstatic to start a year of cheering on our football team together.

Choosing to try out one more time would shape my story in ways I never could have predicted. Not making the team during my seventh- and eighth-grade tryouts seemed like the end of my life at the time. It taught me that things you think will not happen to you can and do, in fact, happen. Mother's words of reassurance then still stand out over a decade later: "No matter what, the sun will rise tomorrow." As she said these words, the sun was actually setting. I have always been very literal, so it gave me a chance to think more deeply about what she was saying, and this image and encouragement stuck.

Because I had the perseverance to keep fighting for a spot on the team, I went on to spend the next three years cheering for my school. During those three years, I was forced to push through difficult circumstances, work hard with others, and remain determined against the odds. Little could I have imagined how much I'd need these skills in the near future, or how closely something that seemed trivial to many would come to resemble my battle between life and death.

My tenth-grade year, I made the high school cheer squad. I was loving every minute of high school, including being in a new building that housed tenth through twelfth grades, sitting with the older kids at lunch, and having a block schedule of four classes daily. Cheer practice was during fourth block, and I loved being around the older, senior girls who soon became some of my closest friends. Friday nights found me cheering on the sidelines and socializing afterward.

I was able to score a part-time job cleaning and performing secretarial duties at a local physical therapy rehabilitation center. I turned 16 and learned to drive. I went on my first date. I cheered Maddi on as she and the girls' basketball team made it to the state tournament. I studied to raise my ACT score. Between a buzzing social life, school, cheer, and work, I barely slept. It was then that I developed my love for being busy.

Life was great, but despite having so many blessings and

loving all of the activities that particular season of life brought me, I found myself with a classic teenage attitude and a dose of negativity. I would like to say that I expressed my gratitude for all of the blessings I had, but in actuality, I was not the best at expressing gratitude. I didn't know life without the comforts and privileges that I was fortunate to have. I didn't realize it, but I had never experienced any true form of hardship.

During the summer between sophomore and junior year, I began to experience pain in my left hip. At first it was mild, but it persisted.

My paternal grandfather, Sam, is a physician, so I asked him to have a look. He concluded that it was likely an injury and advised me to take ibuprofen and use a heating pad to try to reduce some of the inflammation.

In June I went to summer camp, and with the help of ibuprofen and a heating pad, the mysterious pain faded. Once summer camp ended and I returned home, my family and I decided I must have pulled a muscle. A few weeks passed, and the mysterious hip pain disappeared from my body and from my memory.

When mid-July rolled around, my family packed up our car and headed to Florida for a beach vacation. My little brother Andrew was 10, and Bre was 14. I was 16 but felt much older and more mature than that. I spent the week sprinting, swimming, and playing with my siblings on the hot Florida shore. When it was time to depart, we began the long drive home. During the drive, my left hip felt stiff. I rolled onto my right side to ease it, but as the day went on, the discomfort progressed into pain. It continued to bother me the following day, but after a few days, the pain faded once more.

The following week, it was time for cheer camp. This was when we learned our routine that we would perform at competitions, including the State Cheer Competition. This routine was particularly important, as we were the reigning title holders. During the days leading up to cheer camp, practices were rigorous, and we only had a one-day break. On that day, I experienced pain like I had never felt before. Rooted deep in my left hip, it ran sharply down the side of my leg. The pain was constant and magnified when I attempted to sit. With every bend of my hip, I wanted to cry.

Sam examined me again and decided I needed to see another doctor. The following morning, Mother took me to a local family physician. I lay in the car on my right side because the pain was too intense to sit in the waiting room, so intense that Mother had to wait inside in my place. Eventually, when the nurse called my name, Mother walked outside to assist me with getting out of the car and helping me hobble inside. After explaining my symptoms to the doctor and following a complete examination, he came up short on an explanation, let alone a diagnosis.

The following day, I went to cheer camp. Halfway through the practice, my eyes were streaming tears of pain. I explained it to my cheer coach, Mrs. Renfrow. She wrinkled her brows, likely worried for both the routine and for me, before nodding with acceptance. As a result of my pain and failure to perform my best, our guest choreographer placed me on the far back row of the routine in case I needed to be cut later in the season. At home after practice, I pulled my bed covers over my head and cried in pain all night.

The following morning, Mother took me to see a third doctor. He felt that it was an iliotibial (aka IT) band injury caused by the tumbling and jumping in my cheerleading practices. Along with a script for pain medicine, I was encouraged to alternate heat and ice.

For the rest of the week, I was so medicated that Mother had to drive me to practice. If you have never competed in a state cheer competition, it might be difficult to understand why I could not miss choreography week, despite being on pain medicine around the clock. If I was going to be on the mat at the competition, I needed to be on the mat during choreography week. So, I pushed through.

My parents and I decided it would be a good choice to see an orthopedic doctor. Mother was able to get me an appointment with Dr. Mitchell, who had treated me when I broke my elbow in seventh grade for—you guessed it—a cheerleading injury. He had also treated my sister for multiple broken hand injuries throughout her softball years. By my appointment at the end of the week, my hip pain had once again faded. I made the decision to cancel, hopeful that I was on the mend.

Not long after, my junior year of high school began. I managed to get through many Friday nights of cheering and rigorous, daily cheer practices with little pain. I believed that my injury was healing.

In November, the hip pain returned. This time, worse. I rated it eight out of ten on the pain scale, saving nine for something like childbirth or a severely broken leg. This was the worst pain I had experienced to date, but I did not want to waste my ten, which I reserved for something crazy like having a limb amputated with no pain medication. We scheduled another appointment to see Dr. Mitchell. Once he examined me, he agreed it was an IT band injury and decided I needed to start physical therapy.

Some days I breezed through my PT exercises with no difficulty. Others I could barely do modified versions. This pattern ran parallel with my performance ability in cheer. Some days I was able to tumble. Others I was hardly able to stand.

I began seeing Dr. Mitchell regularly. Soon, he decided it was not an IT band injury, but rather a damaged labrum. With this new diagnosis, I continued doing physical therapy and added cortisone shots into my treatment plan. They would give me great relief, but not before immediate, extraordinary pain. Since I was eventually experiencing relief, we chalked up the initially increased pain to my tendency to be dramatic.

One evening in December, my parents were out of town for a couple hours, and I was in charge of keeping an eye on Bre and Andrew. Suddenly, the pain hit. This time, it was stronger. I felt lightheaded. I decided to pick up the pizza I had ordered for us before I felt any worse. In retrospect, it was not a smart idea to drive while feeling lightheaded, but my 16-year-old self did not think in the way that I do now. I managed to pick up the pizza, but throughout the evening the dizziness worsened, and I developed a fever. We brushed it off as me being coincidentally sick and having what we called a "flare up" in my hip at the same time. My parents and I made no correlation between the two, only thinking it was ironic that I was sick and injured at the same time.

The new year came, and I continued to have hip pain on and off, always at the most inconvenient times. Once it was so unbearable that I snuck into the school bathroom to call Daddy so that he could bring pain medicine. My classmates in biology noticed my loopiness and my incessant laughing as a result of the pills and still don't let me live that day down.

As the pain flipped on and off, so did my ability to cheer. At times, my cheer coach and my teammates questioned the reality of my pain, because one day I'd be doing back handsprings and the following day I couldn't walk. I grew exceedingly frustrated because the pain was legitimate. Reflecting, I don't blame others for having their doubts. If the situation were reversed, I would likely doubt their pain as well. Still, it was beginning to make me question the scale of the pain and even question myself. I began to doubt my pain tolerance and wondered if I was letting my inner drama queen take over.

By January, the pain was at an all-time high. Dr. Mitchell decided I needed surgery to repair the damaged labrum in my hip. After discussing the importance of my approaching senior cheer tryouts, he agreed that I could wait to have the surgery immediately after, in time to be healed and ready for late summer competition practices. I needed to have an MRI of my hip to see how extensive the damage was, but because the surgery would not be until March, we scheduled the MRI for February. The plan was to limp me along through tryouts until surgery with cortisone shots and physical therapy.

During this period, it was time for another ACT exam. Throughout the exam, I was extremely uncomfortable sitting at my desk. I guessed on several of the questions, struggling to focus with the nagging reminder of my hip pain. When the exam was over, Mother inquired how I felt about it. I shared how uncomfortable I had been and that "it was probably the worst ACT I have ever done." When the results came in, I was shocked to find out that I had raised my highest score. Looking back, I am so grateful that the higher score was part of God's larger plan, as unbeknownst to me, that would be my last time taking the ACT.

5

The annual Nashville High School Football Banquet was just around the corner. Comparable to the portrayal of the town of Dillon on the TV show *Friday Night Lights*, the closest thing you will find to Texas football outside of Texas, our entire town of Nashville, Arkansas, revolves around high school games, and we are known for winning.

Our mascot, the mighty Scrapper, can be perplexing to outsiders, but I love explaining its meaning. It's not a physical mascot, but rather a fighting spirit. The entire community embodies this fighting spirit when we show up to "The Hill," where our stadium is located, on Friday nights.

The sport is so important in our town that instead of the coaches giving out awards during our annual Sports Banquet in May—when all the other teams receive their awards, including when I received my state championship ring for cheerleading—we hold a special banquet just for football. All of the football players, cheerleaders, and homecoming court members attend, along with parents and fans. The dress is cocktail-style in contrast to the casual sundresses that are typically worn at the sports banquet.

For months in advance, I'd had my junior football banquet outfit planned: a hot pink, shimmery cocktail dress with tall black heels. I stand 5'3" and never, ever wore a dress or skinny jeans without heels.

On the day of the banquet, my hip was bothering me, and ultimately, I was forced to make the decision to wear flats. I am not sure if I was more horrified or embarrassed. All of my friends were shocked to see me wearing flats and took it as a sign that I was in true pain. I attended the banquet with my friend David, and the evening was complete with pictures, corsages, boutonnieres, and dinner, but there was a dark cloud over what should have been a cheerful night.

As my friends, teammates, and peers began to grasp the severity of the pain, it only worsened. A TENS machine was tucked into my bloomers when I cheered. I kept Icy Hot patches wrapped around my thigh. One evening while cheering at a basketball game, I took one of the pills prescribed for when pain became unbearable. With my busy schedule, I had barely eaten all day. That evening, I learned the importance of not taking pain medicine on an empty stomach. I spent the halftime of the girls' game vomiting in the restroom. When my cheer coach, Mrs. Renfrow, learned that I was sick, she sent me home before the boys' game.

All I could do was cuddle up in bed with my chihuahua, Pandora, and try to sleep away the nausea, the pain, and the disappointment.

6

Having never had any sort of scan done other than an X-ray, I wasn't sure what to expect when I stepped into the room with an MRI machine at its center. I was instructed to lie on a table that led into a large, circular tube. As the tech made sure my body was centered, he informed me I could either place my hands on the sides of my body or behind my head. I chose the latter. Here's a hot tip: *Never* lie for an MRI with your hands cupped behind your head. Your arms will get stiff, and you won't be allowed to move them, so you'll probably feel like you're about to lose it.

Once the tech had my body positioned, I began to slide backwards into the tube. In my head, I tried to count as high as I could, hoping that eventually I would fall asleep. Instead, my mind drifted to how I ended up in this noisy machine in Texarkana.

My parents, Andrew, and Maddi all accompanied me to

my appointment. Bre was not able to attend because she had to cheer at a junior high basketball game that evening. Maddi thoughtfully offered to come with me to my MRI. Looking back, I'm so grateful for her presence that day, as I would need her more than ever before.

When we arrived at the hospital, I signed in at the front desk in the waiting room lobby. The receptionist informed Mother that I had to go to an upper level floor for an injection. Knowing my great fear of needles, Mother only allowed what she had to—that we needed to go to the upper floor.

When we stepped off the elevator, I heard the new receptionist murmur something about an injection. While waiting to be called back, I questioned Mother. After I practically pulled her teeth, she told me I needed an injection in my hip. As the words left her lips, my heart sank. I could run. I could plea with the nurse. I could fight it. I could refuse to be still. None of these options made sense, though. The more I tried to come up with an out, the more she and Maddi attempted to reason with me. By pinching my arms, they tried to show me how "unpainful" the needle would be, but with every little pinch, I felt a fresh wave of dread.

As I squirmed in the stiff waiting room chair, Maddi and Mother giggled at my strange antics. With each laugh, I became more worked up. I wanted to escape the injection, to escape the laughing. Jumping up out of my chair, I scanned the room. Finding no way out, I ran to the nearest corner and pressed my back against the wall. I crumpled to the floor and burst into frantic tears.

Then, I was a drama queen who absolutely hated needles. If I were to receive the same injection today, I wouldn't even flinch. My smile would not break, and I might even make a joke to the nurse as it happened. I might even tell her this story.

Eventually my name was called, and Daddy walked back with me. Despite my theatrics, I made it through the injection and returned to the floor where my MRI was to be done. When it was finally time to go back for the scan, I was handed two gowns to change into, one for the front and one for the back. The tech told Mother and me that the MRI would last approximately 45 minutes.

As my arms began to cramp, minutes were lifetimes. Time warped because I had no way of tracking it. *How long have I been in the machine?* Not too long, I convinced myself.

It never crossed my mind that something could be terribly wrong.

Apparently after about an hour and 15 minutes, Mother asked the receptionist at the front desk how much longer it would be until the MRI was done, and the receptionist informed her I was almost finished.

The table slid out of the machine. I asked the new tech standing over me if the scan was over.

"Almost," she said, "but I need to inject more dye. The first injection wore off." This time, the dye was injected into my arm instead of my hip. Not knowing much about scans or dye, I didn't realize this was abnormal.

After the tech completed my second injection, I slid back into the loud tube and lay there for about 15 minutes. When the table slid out of the tube once again, the tech instructed me to go upstairs—that Dr. Mitchell wanted to see me. I recalled it being Dr. Mitchell's surgery day, so that was odd, but I shrugged it off and changed back into my clothes.

The orthopedic clinic was a familiar place because I had visited several times with hip pain, a broken elbow, and my sister's broken hands. This visit was different though. For one thing, the clinic was mostly vacant, excluding a nurse and a front desk receptionist. The hall smelled stoutly of cleaning supplies. The lights were off in all of the clinic rooms.

As we entered one, the nurse turned the lights on, told us Dr. Mitchell would be with us soon, and left. The crisp paper lining the patient's table crinkled as I plopped down. My parents followed closely behind. Maddi and Andrew sat in the waiting room.

Daddy quietly sat and patiently waited. Mother and I conversed about our expectations of what news Dr. Mitchell would bring when he entered the room. We both figured that he was going to want to pick a date for a surgery. Mother had forgotten her planner, and we were trying to remember specific dates, such as senior cheer tryouts and spring break, so that we could fit in the surgery accordingly.

Through the darkness beyond the doorway and into the light of our clinic room, Dr. Mitchell emerged. At first he just stood there as the room filled with a faint humming.

As if each word had been carefully planned, he spoke slowly. "I have bad news. We found a mass. If you'll come into the hallway, we can look at the imaging screen."

Except for the paper that crinkled harshly when I stepped down from the exam table, we followed him quietly into the hallway without words or glances. On the screen was the MRI of my pelvis. Like something out of an anatomy textbook, it felt foreign, but to my untrained eyes, nothing looked off.

Dr. Mitchell used a lot of words that didn't make sense to me. My seventeen-year-old brain thought a mass was a hole, not a tumor-like growth. Dr. Mitchell did not use the word "cancer," so I didn't process the severity of the situation. He did use the word "chemotherapy" when speaking of future possibilities. I was not comprehending much of what he was telling us.

I fed from the energy my parents were giving off. Mother began crying. Daddy firmly put his hand on my shoulder. "We'll go anywhere in the world and do what we need to do to take care of you."

Little did I know how I would cling to the hope in this statement for years to come. My brain had not fully grasped what was unraveling, but I knew that the possibility of having to travel far meant something was terribly wrong.

I was standing still, yet the room was whirling around me in a blur of colors.

The next thing I knew, Dr. Mitchell was escorting us down the hall. He wrote me a prescription for painkillers and instructed me not to do any activity too strenuous—no more tumbling, not even riding a four-wheeler. His concern was the mass location and its potential to cause a break in my leg.

Further testing would need to be done, and because of my age, I needed to go to a children's hospital.

He left us on a semi-uplifting note, saying, "I've had one other patient similar to you. She's from Oklahoma. An athlete. And she's doing well now."

Dr. Mitchell wished me well, and my parents and I shambled through the waiting room door to exit the clinic. Immediately, I asked Maddi, "Where's Andrew?"

Instead of answering, her gaze locked onto the tears in my eyes. "What's wrong?"

I wasn't quite sure why I was crying. My thoughts were not moving as fast as my emotions.

Andrew walked around the corner. I tried to dry my tears quickly. "Where were you?"

"The bathroom."

Maddi gave me the look. The look that meant she knew something was wrong. I knew too. I just didn't know what.

At the elevator, I mumbled under my breath, "I don't know. Let's just go to the car."

I climbed into my mom's Tahoe with Andrew while Daddy explained to Maddi what we had learned. Mother called her dad, my PaPaw. I imagine PaPaw inhaled a deep breath and gave some words of encouragement to Mother. He always seems to have the right words. He's strong, not just because he's six-foot-nine, but because he always knows how to roll with bad news.

Next, they called Daddy's parents, Sam and Suzanne. Sam was preparing to begin one of his many 24-hour emergency department shifts at our local hospital in my hometown, and they made plans for us to stop by the hospital that night.

Finally, my parents called Maddi's parents, Steve and Leslie. I remember Leslie offering to come pick us up and take us to Maddi's house, but we politely declined. Instead, we wanted to go to Texas Roadhouse for buttered rolls and the cheese fries we'd been dreaming about all day. My parents were shocked that Maddi and I still wanted cheese fries in light of the news we'd just received, but I was ready for this celebratory kickoff to our February winter break.

Upon arriving at the restaurant, we promptly ordered the cheese fries. Over the course of our meal, my parents asked if I was okay with the idea of them posting on social media what we had learned from Dr. Mitchell. I instantly protested and declined the idea without much thought. After all, hadn't they raised me with the mindset to not air my dirty laundry?

My dad had a solid point though. "If we share with others, they can be praying for you." Mother agreed.

I believed in prayer, so I couldn't argue against that. But the thought of needing prayers scared me.

We decided to hold off on posting until we had a little more information, but I agreed that once we had it, sharing felt like the right thing to do. (I find it slightly ironic that all these years later I'm sharing all of the private, personal details from this period in my life without a second thought.)

I had no clue how many people would pray for me in the days and years to come. All I knew was that I needed some form of healing, and prayers would lead me to that through God's mighty hand. Even today, I still cannot completely fathom the number of prayer warriors I have had over the last few years, but I will be forever grateful for those who have taken the time to invest in my journey and pray for my healing and peace for my family and for me.

After leaving Texas Roadhouse, my parents seemed to be in a haze. While Maddi and I were busy joking in the back seat and Andrew was blissfully unaware of the situation, Mother slumped against the passenger seat, and Daddy stared vacantly over the highway. Maddi and I talked about the latest high school gossip, and I bragged as I made a new record on Candy Crush. Daddy called his Uncle Larry, who had recently retired as a radiologist in the same clinic where I had my MRI. He agreed to look at the MRI.

When we arrived home, I asked Mother if Maddi and I could meet a couple of friends in town.

"Are you sure that's what you really want to do?"

I quickly nodded.

"Why don't you just stay in tonight?"

"No, everybody is waiting for us. Can we please go?"

Mother pressed her lips together and nodded her head. She later told me that she felt like crawling in a hole.

When we arrived in town, I hopped in a friend's truck. At one point, I briefly told my friends about my day and casually shared that I may have cancer before shrugging it off and moving on to a new topic of conversation.

That night, I slept in my parents' bed. Mother stayed up the entire night.

7

Waiting is the hardest. Around 9 a.m. the morning after Dr. Mitchell told us about the mass, I was sitting in the family room with my parents in a foggy state of exhaustion when I heard a knock at the door. A familiar face peered through the door's window. It was Mrs. Renfrow, my faithful cheer coach.

Following hugs for the entire family, Mrs. Renfrow shared that she had been trying to call me all morning and that after several unanswered calls, she decided to just come visit and find out if there was truth to the rumors swirling around town. Mother explained to her what little knowledge we had about the unforeseeable future.

My parents shared an update from Uncle Larry and that he and my cousin Josh, his grandson and another radiologist in the family, believed it was Ewing's Sarcoma. At this point they were still referring to it as "Ooing's Sarcoma," which sounded like gibberish to me, and I even misunderstood and thought this was a type of bone infection rather than its true meaning: bone cancer. We discussed the upcoming cheer tryouts for my senior year. We even talked about my little sister being old enough to try out and the possibility that I might not be able to try out at all.

Mrs. Renfrow stayed long enough to make each of us feel loved, but without overstaying her welcome. From that point on, countless friends and family members would reach out, call, visit, and provide support in multiple ways. I had so many loved ones step up to champion me that I could write an entire book on Scrapper community support alone. Mrs. Renfrow stands out, though, because she was the first person there for me, and she never stopped rallying around my family.

At the time, I don't think I fully recognized the meaning of Mrs. Renfrow being the first person at my doorstep. Today, I don't doubt one bit that her visit was crucial in preparing my mind to fight a looming, dark battle.

8

Mother and I prepared for the appointment with Arkansas Children Hospital's orthopedic surgeon, Dr. Corey Montgomery, by making sure we had a detailed timeline of my symptoms and everything we had done in an attempt to treat them. The night before, we stayed in a Little Rock hotel. I was more excited about a planned visit to The Container Store while in the city than I was nervous about my appointment. I chose sushi for dinner, and while eating, we discussed making the first post on Facebook to officially share and address the situation.

We had told most of our friends and family, and word was spreading quickly, but this was the first public documentation. Daddy did not have any form of social media at the time, but he gave input on choosing the right words. Mother posted this update to her Facebook page, and I immediately shared it: *"Please pray for our precious Kaden as she is having some health problems. Her orthopedic doctor has found a mass in her hip and is sending us to Children's in the morning to meet with a specialist. Please pray for our sweet girl to get a good report and that this mass is easily treatable. We will update as we know more and appreciate any prayers."*

The next morning, I sat in the waiting room among young children who played with toys while I typed away on my laptop. I took a momentary break to tweet, announcing to my classmates who followed me on Twitter to please inform Mr. Horne, my high school science teacher, that I was at the doctor's office working on my junior year chemistry homework and preparing for an upcoming test.

After a tech had taken my vitals and I was shown to a clinic room, I sat waiting with my parents. This was when the waiting really kicked in. Once Dr. Montgomery made his way to my clinic room, I noted that he appeared to be young, distinguished, and sharply dressed. Even his glasses matched his aesthetic.

After discussing my symptoms, he immediately went to work scheduling a biopsy in the OR, a full body bone scan, a CT of my pelvis, and some lab work. Because we were fitting so many tests into one day and they were not planned ahead of time, it was a rush from one test to another.

First, I went upstairs to my overnight room on a stepdown surgical floor. The nurse attempted to draw blood from my left arm. She struggled to get a good draw and had to move the needle around quite a bit. I struggled to stay still, fixating on the ceiling above me. I recall chatting about how good her eyeliner was and the skills she clearly had to apply such a clean line. It was all merely a distraction, and my parents could not help but chuckle.

Next, I was whisked down to the OR, where I met Dr. Braswell. She performed a biopsy of the mass on my left hip. This was my first experience with laughing gas. As the medicine set in and the cackling fits crept on, it felt like the world was disappearing fast, yet moving in slow motion. I held half of a conversation with one of the OR nurses in the room. I could feel her holding my hand and rubbing my palm as I drifted away. She complimented my nail polish choice, and I instantly responded in a high-pitched, joking, sassy tone, "My nail girl, Macy, did them. I was like, 'Macy, can you fit me in today?' and she was like, 'Yeah, girl, come on!'"

I heard the nurses and doctors surrounding me laugh and joke as my chest felt lighter and I faded away.

The post-op nurses made sure I was recovering well. It was not long before they wheeled me to the radiation center of the hospital. I still needed a full-body bone scan and a CT of my pelvis.

The bone scan was first. As I was pushed into the room with the large camera heads and a long, flat bed, I met my radiology tech, Ashley. She had long dark hair, and glasses framed her face. I would see her many times, both while getting bone scans and visiting the nuclear medicine lab, so we became friends.

When I stood up from the wheelchair, I hobbled over to the bed of the machine and noticed a large bloodstain at the bottom of my hospital gown. I knew the blood was from my biopsy, but it grossed me out. Just the mention of the word "blood" made me extremely squeamish, and the sight of it over-whelmed me. Ashley noticed my reaction and quickly grabbed me a fresh gown to slip into.

That first bone scan was long, but exhausted from all of the day's activities and still fresh out of sedation, I was able to nap. The CT scan only took about 10 minutes.

After the scans, I was taken back to my room on the step-down surgical floor. There had not been a chance to eat all day. When Daddy asked me what I would like for dinner, I chose Slim Chickens. We all joked about how many chicken strips I ate because I was starving.

I didn't sleep that night. Instead, I watched a *Teen Mom* marathon on MTV. Anytime a nurse would enter my room to check on me, I'd quickly turn the volume down. At one point, I didn't hear the nurse come through my door. When I noticed her adjusting the buttons on my IV pole that was pumping me full of fluids, I quickly grabbed the remote to turn it down. She chuckled and reassured me that she didn't mind.

This was the start of many, many reality television mar-athons in the hospital. It became a good mental distraction to see the portrayal of others' lives on reality TV instead of focus-ing on my life within the walls of a hospital, and knowing a new episode would be airing gave me something to look forward to.

I had reality TV shows in the evenings and the TODAY Show in the mornings. TODAY with Kathie Lee and Hoda gave me a reason to wake up many mornings. I especially loved when Jenna Bush-Hager filled in for Kathie Lee. She felt relatable because I loved reading and writing and she was a former English teacher, author, and fellow Southern girl.

Around 6 a.m. the following morning, one of the resident doctors rounded by my room. When he entered, I anxiously sat up, ready to hear the results, naively unaware of the timeline to receive results from a biopsy. Instead, the resident sent me home with instructions to return the following week. I was really confused. This meant I had to wait an entire, agonizing week to find out whether or not I had cancer?

My doctors and parents had not kept any information from me, but I still did not completely understand what cancer and chemo really meant. How could I have? But fully understanding or not, the idea that I was very likely about to be diagnosed with cancer at 17 was beginning to click.

My parents seemed more tense during the car ride than I felt. Perhaps everything was making more sense to them. As Daddy began the two-hour drive home, Mother told me she was going to call Maddi's mom, Leslie. Influenced by the combination of a sleepless night and teen perception, I immediately protested. I wanted to be the one to update my best friend. Mother strongly disagreed. Ultimately, I fell asleep, and she made the call.

Over the years since that day, my mom and I have had

many laughs about this disagreement. Now that I'm older and more mature, I understand that it was best that Maddi's parents were the ones to tell her so that they could comfort her in ways that I couldn't. Since then, I've had to call Maddi many times to relay bad news regarding my health. I wanted so desperately to be the one to tell the news, to be grown up enough for that task. But since then, no matter how many times I have to share bad news with Maddi and my other friends, it never gets easier.

When I first returned home, I met my friend Maggie at McDonald's. Maggie and I have been friends for our entire lives and were both on the high school cheer team. Her dad had just completed treatment for cancer, and her grandpa was in treatment as well. We talked about her knowledge of cancer, the current high school drama, and updates on what was going on within the cheer team. It felt good to catch up on the news, like maybe I would miss a little time and pick right back up where I left off.

For the remainder of the week, I went to classes and basketball games. I was instructed not to cheer, because we didn't know the risks of the mass in my pelvis, but I still dressed out in my uniform and accompanied my squad to games where I vocally cheered from the stands.

I attempted to follow a normal schedule, trying my best to distract myself from the waiting.

9

Delayed due to snow—not at all common in Southwest Arkansas—eventually, the results were back.

On the drive back to Dr. Montgomery's clinic at Arkansas Children's Hospital, Mother explained to me the difference between two words I'd heard thrown around: benign and malignant. There wasn't an easy way to remember it. Benign didn't go with bad. Malignant went with bad.

Once I was seated in a brightly-lit clinic room with Mother and Daddy, Dr. Montgomery entered with a resident at his tail. He sat down on the doctor's rolling stool and greeted me with a firm yet warm handshake, welcoming my parents and me back. He was quick to get to the point.

"Unfortunately, the tumor is malignant," he said, his voice gentle.

Malignant. The one I didn't want. The bad one. I couldn't see Dr. Montgomery's face through my tears. The overwhelming, awful scent of soap and cleaning spray permeated the room. My parents squeezed me tight, muttering words of encouragement.

I could not tell you another word that was said in that clinic room, and I would be willing to bet if you ask my parents, their memory of that moment would be just as fuzzy. While the blur of words droned on, I began to silently mourn the loss of the life I knew. While it was not officially confirmed until Dr. Montgomery said it was, I'd had two weeks since that first MRI to hear the word "cancer" rattle around in my brain. Yet why would it happen to me? Does anyone ever think cancer will actually happen to them? Does any teen ever think they will get cancer? Surely teens don't get cancer.

We left the orthopedic clinic with instructions from Dr. Montgomery to meet my new oncologist in the Hematology-Oncology clinic at 1 p.m. Dr. Montgomery ended that visit with an analogy for me to visually recognize the treatment team that was forming for my care. He said, "I'm in the quarterback position right now, but I'm moving to one of the other starting football positions. This new doctor, Dr. Stine, is going to take over as your quarterback and be in charge of your treatment plan, but I'm still on your team and ready to do surgery if necessary to get rid of the tumor. We are all fighting for you." He sounded so confident. I would continue to cling to his confidence during times of discussion of a possible surgery.

Before departing, my parents and I stopped in the hall to call PaPaw so that he could break the news to my siblings.

We grabbed a quick lunch from the cafeteria. I was in

such an odd state of shock that although I hate salads, I chose the salad bar over the hamburger line. Maybe I chose salad because I thought it might help my body. It was now abundantly clear that my body needed help.

Once we made it to the clinic waiting room, I sat with Mother and Daddy at my sides. The waiting room had a large sign that read "Circle of Friends Hematology-Oncology Clinic." I had heard the word "oncology" enough that it was clear this was the kind of clinic where I was to meet a special cancer doctor. Now, I cannot help but laugh as I recall asking Mother what the word oncology meant.

I then met the incredible Dr. Stine. I always appreciated his pastel, collared shirts which paired well with his silver hair and wire-rimmed glasses.

My primary oncologist at ACH, Dr. Stine specializes in sarcomas, so he was a perfect match to treat my diagnosis: stage 2b Ewing's Sarcoma. My parents and I spent the entire afternoon mesmerized in an intense conversation with him and his specialty nurse, Carol. Even shorter than me, she looked up at me through her glasses when we spoke. The five of us talked stages, treatment plans, and study options, and Dr. Stine explained what to expect when receiving chemotherapy.

When one is diagnosed with Ewing's Sarcoma, the doctor provides a treatment plan or road map. My road map consisted of three phases. Phase One, Induction Therapy, consisted of six rounds of chemo, each inpatient in the hospital for three to six days. Phase Two was called Local Control and consisted of radiation, surgery, or both. Finally, Phase Three was called Consolidation Therapy and consisted of eleven more rounds of inpatient chemo. Because we all agreed that surgery was not necessary to kill my cancer, I was able to start Phase Three when I began Phase Two, meaning that I would continue doing chemotherapy and start radiation therapy after completing round six.

After hours and hours of questions, Dr. Stine looked at my parents and me and said, "No more questions for the day." It was a good thing he stopped us there, because we needed time to absorb such an overwhelming diagnosis and all of the information that came flying in with it.

Dr. Stine respected that I was 17 years old, and he didn't just walk in and begin talking to my parents as if I weren't in the room. He told me that day that there would never be any conversations about me or my health that didn't include me. I didn't have to worry that maybe my parents and doctors were hiding anything. Because of that, a bond of trust was formed that substantially impacted my emotional health for years to come. From that day on, when things would get scary and we were unsure of what was to come, I was never worried. I knew that Dr. Stine would always be honest with me, and that is one of the many reasons that I have great respect for the man.

Before I left the clinic, Dr. Stine said, "I'll come talk to you in the morning in pre-op prep to answer more questions before you have your port placed." It was comforting to know that I'd be seeing him again soon.

Carol then escorted my parents and me to "4K," the inpatient Hematology-Oncology—or "Hem-Onc" for the frequent-flyers, like myself—unit at ACH. Maybe it was better that I didn't realize 4K was about to become my second home. Between the ages of 17 and 21, I'd spend as many nights on 4K as I would in my own bed. I would soon deem 4K the "Hilton of the hospital." It consists of two hallways, 26 private and spacious patient rooms, a mini playroom, a smaller version of a teen room for older patients, two nutrition rooms with snacks and beverages for the patients and families, and a large family house. The family house includes a kitchen area, couches, tables, a flat screen TV, computers and printers, and a laundry room.

I would spend many hours in the family house on 4K, and my family would spend even more hours there as a place to get out of my hospital room while I was taking long naps.

In a way, the people of 4K became my family as well. Besides my real family and close friends who visited, I had to be put in a bubble away from the germy outside world because my immune system was compromised. The nurses, doctors, and other patients became my constant.

Sydney was the first oncology nurse I met.

"So, Sydney, I'm afraid of needles," I shared with a half laugh that barely concealed my deep fear. "Am I going to have a lot of needle pokes?"

She laughed with me and shrugged, but I noticed she avoided the answer. The unsaid answer was yes. Yes, I would have hundreds of needle pokes to come.

10

I had assumed that on the days I was not getting chemo, I would go to school. I was wrong. On the days I wasn't getting transfusions, I would feel ill eighty percent of the time either from the chemo making me heavily nauseated or from weakness due to being low on blood. (Along with my hair cells, the chemo was killing my blood cells.) What I learned over the months to come was that on the few days where I was not symptomatically feeling bad, my immune system would be too weak to be among crowds.

"Chemo will make your white blood cell count drop, and your white blood cells are what fight off infections," Dr. Stine explained. "What do you think some examples of crowds to avoid might be?"

"Concerts?" My mind instantly went to a crowded concert arena, jam packed with people. Initially saddened by this restriction, the reality was I didn't go to concerts often.

"True," Dr. Stine replied, "but there are some others."

Three categories of places I could not go when my white blood cell counts were low were school, church, and Walmart. Growing up in a small town, these were about the only three places I could possibly go, with the exclusion of restaurants, which of course were deemed too crowded as well. To-go food would become my go-to.

As we spoke, I began to realize how much of the life I had known was slipping away.

The day I had my first port placed was another of my early experiences with nitrous oxide—better known as laughing gas. I sang Beyoncé's "Flawless" and "Single Ladies" for the entire operating room. I flung my hands in the air and giggled heavily before passing out to the sound of the surgical team's laughter.

In the following years, I would be sedated over 30 times, two-thirds of those including nitrous oxide. Under its influence, I put on dramatic performances, showered compliments, and received life-saving operations.

That first port was placed deep, causing the nurses to have to use an inch-and-a-half-long needle. This was the longest needle that the clinic kept in stock, and throughout my time with a port, I always noticed how my nurses' faces would drop when I told them what size needle I needed. This was a clear indication that it would be a hard stick.

Prior to surgery, I believed that my port would create a

scenario in which I needed fewer needle pokes, which was not true. Surgically placed beneath the skin of the chest, the port is a round device connecting to a vein that goes directly into the heart. It can be used to draw labs and infuse medicines, blood, and other types of infusions. Over the next four years, I would have three ports and three "double lumen" (meaning it had two internal channels) central lines placed in my chest, each at different times.

When I woke up in post-op, I was extremely sore. My parents were able to come back and see me. When the pain medicine kicked in, I began singing Beyoncé's songs again. I told all of the nurses how much I love Beyoncé and that I wished to meet her. The nurses and the surgical team that spoke with my parents after the surgery shared with them how entertaining I was. Apparently, laughing gas does not always make patients have fun. Sometimes younger kids grow fussy or scared.

Being a 17-year-old patient is different from being a 5- or 12-year-old patient, and this only became more clear as I aged and continued being treated with young kids. While there were obvious differences, and I was not always "textbook" for pediatrics, my doctors were extremely accommodating to keep me comfortable and find the best treatment for my body. They even spoiled me to the point that I became noted for saying, "I never want to go to an adult hospital."

Once I began to sober up from all of the surgery medicines, I was released to go home for a few days before starting chemo. I struggled to get comfortable in the car, as the seatbelt went directly over my chest where my port was freshly placed. The pain was immediate, and with each bump in the road I could feel my whole chest sting. I half-joked, half-begged for Daddy to "not drive bumpy," as if that were an actual possibility when driving on the interstate. It stuck though, and anytime in the future when the roads were uneven or I'd just had some sort of procedure, my family and I would joke about not driving bumpy.

12

Luke, a longtime friend from school, was heavily involved with the school's journalism program and even had a job with our town newspaper. The day after my diagnosis, he immediately texted me with support, followed by proposing an interview for an article. I agreed.

Between having my port placed and starting chemo, I needed to be driven, and Maddi volunteered to drive me to the interview. Maddi sat and listened as Luke asked me questions about my diagnosis and how it was discovered, the treatment I would need, and other questions related to my health outlook.

I felt so thankful that he was taking the time to interview me and told him so repeatedly. "People get cancer all the time," I said. I felt special for getting to be on the front page of the newspaper just for getting cancer. But "people" were adults. We both agreed that it must be unusual that kids get cancer because it was something we'd only heard of in movies like *The Fault in Our Stars.* We believed that kids did not get cancer, because we were not aware that kids get cancer. Then, I became a kid with cancer. I learned how wrong we were, that I was hardly alone, and that actually childhood cancer is not rare, it's just not always talked about—all the more motivation to help spread awareness.

After the interview, in honor of one of my last meals out before starting treatment, Maddi and I stopped at a local Mexican restaurant to meet Bre for a late brunch.

Once at Maddi's house, we began getting ready for the evening. We had plans to go to a rodeo with her parents and Brady, her boyfriend at the time. As it tends to go in a small town, I had known Brady my entire life, and we had always been friends. When the three of us hung out, cutting up and joking was inevitable. That night was no different, and they both wanted to make it special for me since it was one of my last nights to do something normal before chemo.

This is when the celebration mindset budded. In the days, weeks, and years to come, I learned to look for any reason to celebrate—something I remain intentional about. I would celebrate days when the cancer had not grown any more, days when I reached remission, days when I completed treatment, and days when I graduated high school, went to college, and moved out. I would also celebrate the small things, like landing good parking spots, driving through Chick-fil-A, watching *The Real Housewives*, scoring a new stick of eyeliner, getting snuggles from my dogs, or spending time with my family. Constant celebrating and positivity are what pushed me through. There will always be bad, but there will always be good too. Sometimes you have to search, but when you do, you'll find it.

My faith in God's insightful will helped me remain positive. Part of my faith in God is trusting that everything happens for the greater purpose. The small things and the big things, the good things and the bad things. Everything connects. I knew early on that good would come from my cancer, I just wasn't sure in what ways.

That weekend I had three things to celebrate: my interview with Luke, time with Maddi and Brady, and getting a new bedroom. While I was at Maddi's house for the weekend, my family worked together to swap Andrew's and my bedrooms. The way my childhood home is laid out, there are enough bedrooms for each of us kids to have our own, but two must share a bathroom. Until this point, my brother had the bigger bedroom and a private bath.

My parents decided to swap our rooms. I was going to be spending a lot of time at home, so they wanted to make me as comfortable as possible. This was also a welcome change because my vision is incredibly bad and has been my whole life. I can't even walk from my bed into my bathroom without contacts or glasses.

In less than 48 hours, my parents moved all of Andrew's and my belongings, painted his room blue and mine pink, tore up the carpet in my new room, and put down hardwood flooring. I even got to put a couch in my bedroom for the days when

I would be too weak to walk to the living room and the nights when I would be so sick that Mother would have to sleep with me in my room. Dr. Stine had warned us this was ahead, and even though I couldn't quite imagine it being true, it seemed best to prepare.

I also set up a blog that weekend, deciding it would be the easiest way to update others on my journey. I did really well at posting updates and sharing my thoughts on life during my treatment for Ewing's, and it kickstarted my love of writing. It was a good hobby and a way to express my thoughts. While many of my posts embarrass me to look back on, they encouraged me to start writing, study English in college, and write this book.

Before starting chemo, Mother took me on a special shopping trip for hospital necessities and comfort items. We were in search of anything I might need to make hospital visits cozier: cute matching pajama sets, fluffy pillows, slippers, and pink floral blankets. Mother suggested I would need what she called "loungewear" aka clothes that are comfortable-yet-cute and not too pajama-y. I had my own set of pillows and blankets that I brought to use instead of the hospital's bedding.

Mother also suggested we have some photographs made before I started chemo. While it was still March of my junior year, I ended up having several sessions of senior pictures, two with my hair and two without. In one of the two sessions with my hair, my wonderful photographer friend Jenna captured some pictures that I treasure dearly. They show innocence in my eyes and portray my body long before a collection of scars, thin hair and baldness, and a damaged leg, each a reflection of the havoc treatment wreaked. While I am grateful to simply be alive and have a body, I am also grateful to have pictures from a time before so much damage.

Two months prior to my Ewing's Sarcoma diagnosis, I received a gift. While it might sound silly, I was thrilled to receive my own set of nice, grown-up luggage. Three matching, bubble-gum pink, hard-shell suitcases excited me, because these appeared more mature and put-together than the overnight totes or childish bags I had previously carried.

When I opened this gift on Christmas morning, I was first ecstatic, then hopeful that I would take a trip soon where I could use my fancy new cases. Little did I know that just two months later, I would begin a period of intense traveling—to the hospital. Those suitcases would take me through nearly four dozen hospital stays, a European vacation, a trip to Disney World, a sister trip to Chicago, a cheerful trip to Vegas, and a few trips to my parents' house after moving out for college.

Even with a limp from nerve damage, I would learn to tug them along behind me. Although I could manage, it was

Daddy who would always unload the car and repack it for my hospital stays. For extended stays, we would learn to request a cart from the hospital's stat team onto which we'd stack my luggage and additional bags. Mother and I would often joke and reference the movie *Steel Magnolias* as Daddy unloaded everything: "I love you more than my luggage."

During my first admission for chemo, we learned the best process for admit day. To be admitted to 4K, you either have to go through clinic or the emergency department. There is no way to directly admit, and both routes require lengthy processes. Just days after receiving an official diagnosis, my parents went with me to the hospital. Unfamiliar with admission, Daddy and I each brought in a couple of suitcases as we walked into the clinic with Mother.

That day, I met Karla, an experienced nurse who became a constant in my life when things were quickly changing. She explained to me that during admission, it might be best to wait until I got to the floor before bringing my luggage in. This way, we would not be lugging it through the clinic and wouldn't have to deal with carrying it back out to the car if I were to not make counts and have to delay chemo. Mother stood in the corner and silently chuckled because she had warned me it was not necessary to bring it in, but I had insisted.

All too soon, it was time for labs to be drawn for the first time through my port. I was still terrified of needles, and the thought of blood made me lightheaded. Karla first accessed my port, and despite my nervousness, she did a great job. There may have been a silent tear or two as I felt the needle press through my skin and the port resist, then finally pop forward. For months, Karla would be the only person I'd allow to access my port. I finally let another nurse try when Karla got a new job and I was forced to broaden my horizons. Ironically, I would go on to let new nurses access my port as a learning opportunity, warning them I was a hard stick and reassuring them when they inevitably missed on their first try. The veteran nurses liked me to volunteer for those fresh out of nursing school because my deep port was a difficult stick, making for great practice. Eventually, I'd let my parents and Bre access my port, and even do it myself.

Once Karla had drawn my labs that first day, my parents and I headed to the unit. By the time I was admitted to the hospital and settled into my room—room 10—it was nearing 7 p.m. As anyone who has spent any time in a hospital knows, shortly before 7, things come alive, the sign of shift change. ACH tries to avoid starting chemo right before shift change, so my parents went to get takeout for dinner, and I waited for my night shift nurse to arrive.

My knowledge of how chemo works was so limited that I actually thought Dr. Stine would be administering the medicine himself. In actuality, it would be a nurse who would gown, double glove, and mask to spike the bags of poison through the tubes connected to the port in my chest. It would be a nurse who would bring the anti-nausea drugs and the blue bags for when my stomach could not keep anything down. It would be a nurse who would sit with me for hours while my parents were trying to catch a bit of sleep or a shower, or were out getting food for me. It would be a nurse who would explain the doctors' big, mysterious words. It would be a nurse who would help bathe me when I was too weak and who would call the doctor-on-call time after time, because she *knew* something was not right. It would be a nurse who would help me come up with solutions to treatment complications and who would lie next to me in my hospital bed after a long day of bad news. It would be a nurse who would bend over backward caring for me, and then ask my parents if they needed anything as well.

That first night shift nurse's name was Amber. Her long blonde hair, shiny blue eyes, and soft voice convinced me that she is an angel in disguise from Heaven. All of my 4K nurses are precious, but Amber will always be special. I'm not sure which nurse was team-leading that day and made the assignment, but I have a feeling they knew what they were doing by giving Amber to the freshly-diagnosed patient. We stayed up chatting and quickly bonded. She answered my lingering questions and made me feel comfortable with my first chemo infusion. She took the time to explain what she was doing as she hooked me up to the IV. I have never had a bad nurse on 4K, but Amber definitely set the bar high that night. I saw Jesus in Amber, and she would also provide support for my faith in God. She was a setting stone for how I viewed cancer, chemo, and being at the hospital, and she has the power to brighten the darkest of dark days, helping me to always see the good.

Two days of chemo went by, and the side effects set in: extreme nausea, violent vomiting, brutal hot flashes, and mild fatigue. (I would come to learn the difference between mild and severe fatigue.) As a girl who did not previously like ponytails, my "hospital hair" was often pulled up on top of my head, a mini fan and a gray bucket at my side for when the nausea got too heavy. I had the option between it and the plastic, disposable, blue bags to which I quickly switched. They were more practical because they could easily be thrown out with no mess, and the nurses could record the volume as they tracked all of my ins and outs while at the hospital.

Blue bags were easy to keep in a purse, on my nightstand, in medicine bags, and in cars, which was good because I'd need them in all those places. Maddi even kept a couple in her car in case I was with her after chemo. I recommend blue bags to everyone, not just the sick. We all get stomach bugs or car sickness from time to time. They're real lifesavers.

During this time of such newness, I met my first child life specialist, Emily. Not many years older than me, she is a fellow lover of all things pink and sparkly. As a child life specialist, Emily's job is to make patients feel more comfortable with the hospital environment, as well as to help educate patients and their families on procedures and treatment plans. Emily was great at never treating me like a kid, and I always enjoyed just hanging out with her.

The day we met, she casually asked me if I was interested in the Beads of Courage Program. Beads of Courage is a national program to help motivate children in active treatment for a variety of diseases, including cancer. Patients simply fill out a card with all of the medical tasks they have completed, such as surgery, chemo, needle pokes, and transfusions. For each treatment task on the card, there is a coordinating colored bead. Patients can string their beads, and at the end of treatment, they have something to show for all they have been through. Initially, it seemed kind of silly, but I was open to the idea. It turned out to be something I love. All of my beads are in chronological order, and I have a strand for each of my diagnoses. I can look at my beads and recognize a specific period of time and what I went through medically. They are the best storytellers. Far better than I could ever describe verbally, they offer a visual display of what I have been through.

14

While I began to feel the physical side effects of the chemo, after a couple of days, I also felt homesick. I expressed concern to Mother, unsure how I would stay in the hospital for week-long rounds of chemo, of which there were seventeen. I was only at the beginning, and already I was stir crazy and missed my home, friends, and family. Mother provided reassurance that I most definitely *could* do it and that I *would* do it. She reminded me that my siblings and PaPaw were coming to visit on Saturday, just a couple of days away, and that gave me something to look forward to.

When Saturday came, I was thrilled to see the rest of my family. Andrew was not allowed to come to 4K because the hospital policy did not allow visitors under age 12 on the unit during flu season. So, my parents pushed me in a wheelchair down to the hospital's first floor by the Riverbend Café so I could visit him and Bre, who was waiting there with him. I felt excited yet worried for my siblings to see me, as I knew I looked frail and sick.

When it was time for chemo again, Mother, Bre, and Pa-Paw came upstairs with me while Daddy took Andrew out for entertainment. When we got to my room, my sister climbed in my hospital bed with me and let me snuggle up to her. Bre is not always a touchy-feely person and normally would not do this, but she knew I was sick and needed her, so she rested with me. A few inches taller than me, her legs stretched down farther in the bed than mine, and her dark hair spread across our shared pillow, her light green eyes peering back at me. We have since spent countless days and nights in a hospital bed together, me being careful to not snuggle her too much and her being careful to not get caught in all my tubes of IV medications. We watched *Cinderella* that afternoon, followed by more Disney movies as I dozed in and out.

My nurse hooked my chemo up as I shared my new knowledge with Bre and PaPaw about how the chemo works. I explained that my nurse has to wear gear to protect her from it. I turned back to Bre and noticed she was peering at the lines of tubing with big eyes, similar to how I imagine I looked during the first dose.

PaPaw and Mother sat on the couch next to us and watched every breath I took. PaPaw was always so positive. Anytime I turned to him, he nodded with reassurance. He typically wore blue jeans or overalls that were blue like his eyes, and that day he wore jeans.

I was sad when the weekend was up and the rest of my family had to leave, but I could look forward to going home the following day and being reunited again.

On Sunday, I finished the first round of chemo. On Monday, I was discharged after receiving a shot of Neulasta, a drug that is supposed to help boost white blood cell counts. I received this shot after each round of chemo in treatment for Ewing's and would go on to take its sister drug, Neupogen, in the future. I still had a fear of needles but was working on toughening up since it was clear that they were going to be pervasive in my future.

The car ride home was hard due to nausea and vomiting. Maddi and my friend Anna came to visit and check on me, and Mrs. Renfrow did as well. She brought the funds earned from the first of what would be many fundraisers she led for me, as well as a pot of fresh, homemade soup. It was the creamiest potato soup ever, and it warmed me. It was better going down than it was coming up.

We quickly learned that just because the chemo infusion stops does not mean the side effects do. Nausea and vomiting can persist several days after chemo, usually just until you begin to feel the impact of low blood counts. The counts being measured included hemoglobin (my red blood cells, which relate to anemia), white blood cells (which fight infection), and platelets (which prevent bleeding and excessive bruising).

I learned that if I finished chemo on Sunday, I would feel queasy on Monday and Tuesday. Wednesday would be better. Thursday would bring extreme muscle aches. Friday would bring low counts. Luckily, my follow-up appointments between chemo treatments were always on Wednesdays, based around Dr. Stine's scheduling.

We also learned that I would require anti-nausea meds those first couple of days post-chemo, starting in the parking lot and going around the clock, even through the night. Sometimes, if I was lucky, the scheduling of my IV anti-nausea medicines in the hospital would line up and I could get a dose right before being discharged to go home.

By Tuesday, I was still extremely weak and nauseated. For lunch, Daddy drove to town to get my favorite cheeseburger, with pickles and ketchup only. He brought back a Dr. Pepper as well, and I'm pretty sure each sip touched my soul. I mustered all of my strength to walk from my bed to the dining table. Despite the nausea, my love of food pushed through, and I ate it all. It took all of my energy, and I returned to bed promptly after. My mom was so encouraging and kept telling me how proud she was of me for getting out of bed and eating the whole meal. While it sounds silly to be proud over something so routine, it boosted my confidence because it had taken everything I had.

Wednesday was significantly better, and while I rested in bed most of the day, I had enough energy to shoot the outdoor session of my senior pictures that evening. For the first time in days, I felt good enough to get out of bed, put on real clothes, fix my hair, and draw on my eyeliner.

The following week, before round two of chemo, it was time for cheer tryouts. I had planned on attending the mock tryouts, which are like a rehearsal for friends and family the day prior to tryouts, but between feeling crummy and needing to avoid the crowded audience, I was not able to. It was important to me to be there in support of my friends and my sister during her first high school tryout.

Mrs. Renfrow let me sit in on the actual tryouts as long as I agreed to step out when it was Bre's turn. I complied, but I still stood at the door and listened from the hallway. Maggie, a graduating senior cheerleader and my friend who met me at McDonald's after my biopsy, gave me the full report later. When I re-entered the room, I sat next to Brooke, a graduating senior. I felt my eyes fill with tears, but I didn't want Brooke and Maggie to see. As stressful as cheer was at times, this was when it really hit me that I would not be cheering on the sidelines my senior year and that my sister and I would never cheer together in high school. We had looked forward to being in high school and cheering together for a long time, and I was watching that dream fade away. As I tried to choke back tears, Maggie and Brooke hugged me, loving me silently.

15

I returned to ACH a few days later for my second round of che-mo. Overnight, my hair began to fall out in clumps. It happened so fast. It made sense to cut my hair because it was falling out and sticking to my clothes. Within 24 hours, there were visibile bald patches on my scalp.

After Mother cut my hair, she told me how cute it looked, and I even thought for a minute that I agreed with her. A style I would have hated in any other circumstance I suddenly agreed was cute, mostly because I was so happy that I still had some hair.

Mother carefully placed the cut hair into a Ziplock. When I raised the bag to the light, it looked like a head full. Eventually, the hair that was cut from my head that day would be framed in a shadowbox with a big pink cheer bow.

A few hours after my haircut, Daddy surprised me and brought in a pair of clippers so I could shave his head while

Mother headed to the mall for new accessory options. The nurses brought towels to wrap around his neck, and I went to work shaving off his dark curls. Somehow, it made me feel better. We had a lot of laughter that day, and he would continue the bald look all through treatment for my first two diagnoses.

While the tears had stopped when the cutting stopped, I could tell my parents knew I was sad to lose what we joked about as being "my lifeline."

When Mother returned from the mall to my hospital room with bags of headbands, hats, and scarves, I thought back to a few weeks before when we'd delved into other cover-up options. Between starting chemo and my hair actually falling out, Mother and PaPaw had taken me to a wig shop. Much more than a grandpa, PaPaw is like my third parent, my sounding board when I have a problem, and my inspiration for life. He shows up for everything, so it is only natural he was with us for wig shopping.

I enjoyed trying on all of the different wigs and playing in front of the mirror. That day I chose eleven wigs, each with a different cut and color. Mother and PaPaw bought all eleven. The short platinum blonde one and a curly red one ended up being two of my favorites.

When it was time to go home the following week, I somehow managed to have enough hair left on my head for Maddi to shave.

Her white Jetta pulled into my parents' driveway, and she stepped out wearing athletic shorts and a T-shirt. For years, Maddi and I had both worn long hair, but hers was wavier and mine was straight. Now, her hair was long and mine was not only short, but it was about to be gone.

Maddi and I headed to the back patio, where my parents joined us. Maddi slowly grabbed the clippers and switched them on. *Buzzzz.* As she shaved my head, she teased that I never wore my hair in a ponytail except for when I cheered. She was right. I hated wearing my hair up because it felt like I wasn't ready for the day and "fixed." I had held this mindset for years. Despite being a night owl, I woke up at 5:30 every single morning in the 8th grade to curl my hair. Being "fixed" was important.

"You always want your hair fixed, and now we are just shaving it all off," she pointed out. We both giggled.

There were no tears that day, only smiles. While I did not want to lose my hair, I had accepted it. I needed to just own it.

Afterward, Maddi and I fixed my makeup so we could take a special selfie to post my new look to Instagram. We sat on my couch, trying to get the perfect angle that showcased my bald head. We ended the night at our friends Brooke and Brady's house. Maddi was dating Brady, and I was close with the brother-sister twin set. They were the first to see me bald. As soon as I stepped into their living room, my friends and their mother, Tammy, began oohing and ahhing.

"I actually have lots of options," I shared. "I can wear a

wig. I already have eleven! Or I can wear a headscarf. And there are so many ways I can tie the scarves. Or I can even do nothing and just go bald. Think how much faster I'll be able to get ready in the morning."

We spent some time playing with the various headscarf styles as Tammy helped me tie them in different ways. Maybe I was trying to see the good in losing my hair. Everyone followed my lead, and we all remained positive.

While I wore wigs a few more times for fun, I learned over time that I had no reason to try and hide my baldness. I definitely caught many strangers' eyes peering with intrigue over the years, but nobody ever said anything hurtful. Eventually, I stopped wearing wigs altogether. I really liked being bald and almost preferred it. Being bald was a reminder of how tough I was. It felt badass.

16

Pet therapy was one of the activities that made the hospital not only bearable but enjoyable. Spending time with dogs in the hospital helped me to not miss my own dog, Pandora, so much. One evening at ACH during pet therapy, I met Taylor and his mother, Angela. I learned that Taylor had osteosarcoma, also a bone cancer similar to my diagnosis. He was one year older than me, and we had Dr. Stine, so we would both go to the clinic on Wednesdays and be admitted to the hospital for chemo together. He frequently wore graphic T-shirts with images of movies or bands he was interested in and often had a grin on his face. He was well-known on 4k for putting on sock puppet shows for the nurses. Taylor was on the autism spectrum and didn't talk much, but he would chat with me. He became my first friend at ACH.

Taylor sang a specific song for each of the chemos that he took. "The Piña Colada Song" by Jimmy Buffet went with

Methotrexate, a yellow, liquid chemo, and he would sing "Rag Doll" by Aerosmith when receiving Doxorubicin, a red chemo infusion.

Once, Taylor came into my room alone. My parents and I quickly noticed that his mom was not with him, which was unusual. A few minutes later, he informed us that she'd gone to the cafeteria. Before long, I heard buzzing. I didn't even know Taylor had a phone, but he pulled one out of his pocket and answered. His mother was on the other end of the line and wanted to know where he was, as she was in his hospital room and it was empty. He said he was in my room, and she walked down the hall to join us. We all had a big laugh because it was not like Taylor to just leave his room on his own, and especially to not tell anyone where he was going.

Taylor's mom soon introduced me to another teenage boy in treatment, Faijon. He often wore white T-shirts and bandanas wrapped around his head. He had a muscular build, and I could tell he was physically strong despite the chemo. Faijon had been finishing his initial treatment for osteosarcoma around the time that Taylor was first diagnosed, nearly a year prior. Faijon had relapsed and was back in treatment. Because he had many younger siblings, he had to stay at the hospital by himself.

Taylor, Faijon, and I spent a lot of time hanging out and passing the time together. My friendships with other patients were beginning to grow.

17

In a town with a population of about six thousand, everybody seems to know everybody. Not everyone fighting cancer is blessed to have a community as amazing as Nashville. My town has provided countless fundraisers for my family and me, stayed updated on any prayer requests, and supported me in ways that nobody could expect. My high school worked with me to make sure I was able to do schoolwork online and graduate with my class on time, with a few college credits even. My senior year, the school superintendent surprised me with the title of honorary cheerleader.

I didn't get any persistent stares at home. Everywhere I would go in town, others would stop to give me a hug and tell me how they had been praying for me. Nashville has made my family and me feel extremely loved.

Around the time of cheer tryouts, Mrs. Renfrow, one of the conductors on my support train, nominated me for a contest with a local publication: *ALT Magazine*'s Athlete of the Year in Southwest Arkansas and Northeast Texas. Mrs. Renfrow's beautiful entry described how I met all of the nomination requirements except one, being an active athlete. After she submitted the nomination, the magazine shared it on Facebook. She wrote:

> "... *For six months, while cheering with her squad and undergoing months of rehab, an ugly tumor as big as [Kaden's] fist had been growing larger and larger on her hip ... While a number of young ladies are spending hours preparing for cheerleading tryouts for the upcoming season, Kaden is spending hours in Arkansas Children's Hospital receiving chemotherapy treatments. As other girls fight for the chance to receive a place on the cheer squad, Kaden will be fighting the ultimate battle: the battle for her life. This disease has taken away her ability to be a Scrapper cheerleader, the one thing that she wanted to do more than anything else ... Instead of spending most of her last year of high school with her classmates, she will continue on her long, hard journey with multiple chemotherapies. ... While cancer has robbed Kaden of almost everything that many little girls look forward to all of their lives, there is one thing that cancer will not rob from Kaden Peebles —her spirit.*"

I was honored that she viewed my pain and struggles in such a positive way.

I will never stop thinking that there's a reason I went eight months with a misdiagnosis of a sports injury. I fully believe it was to toughen and prepare me for the obstacles to come and to teach me about true perseverance. Perhaps Mrs. Renfrow thought she was only pushing me to be better in cheer, but while she was pushing me to be tougher and stronger as an athlete, she was also helping to forge my tenacity and accountability in other aspects of my life. She read my blogs faithfully and bragged once how impressed she was with them. This "small" comment stuck with me for years and built my confidence in writing. She would be one of the first people I told that I was writing this book, and she was super supportive from the early days of drafting.

During my fourth round of chemo, I'd need that toughness. I had tried three types of chemo combinations and was starting the rotation again. The side effects had hit me with a mighty force, and I was incredibly sick with violent vomiting and relentless nausea. I was taking several anti-nausea medications, but not on a schedule. One morning during rounds, Dr. Stine was the oncologist on call, so he entered my room to discuss how I was doing. His eyes looked heavy, and he spoke even softer than usual, probably because he could see how violent the vomiting was and what the nausea was doing to my body. He had seen it for decades in children and teens receiving the same chemo as me. He knew better than anyone.

Calmly and quietly he asked me, "Kaden, do you just want to sleep through this round of chemo? That might be easier."

He had previously warned me that I may want to make

the decision to do this when the chemo made me too sick. I nodded and gave a small smile, knowing that if I could just sleep for the next few days, I would be provided unspeakable relief.

We did not do any sedative medications but made the change to anti-nausea meds. Several of them would make me sleepy and loopy. I was on a constant Zofran drip with a rotation of drugs every three hours around the clock: Ativan, Benadryl, and topical Phenergan. While oral Benadryl typically does not make me sleepy, IV Benadryl works much faster and can make me instantly tired. My parents had to pick up the topical Phenergan from a special compound pharmacy, as the IV version made me too jittery. This chemo cocktail is common in the oncology world.

From that point on, this was my regimen for every round of chemo for Ewing's treatment. It meant that I spent a lot of time feeling more like I was floating than walking while in the hospital. All of my good friends from home have visited me in the hospital to find me high as a kite and have received phone calls from an even more chatty "Kativan," as my nurses would call me when medicated.

One time, when roaming the halls of the oncology unit, Kativan got the bright idea to begin twerking for her nurses. Two nurses in particular, Summer and Krystle, were entertaining my medicated antics and began cheering me on and dancing along. I started music in the hospital hallway and was bobbing my bottom along. At some point, other nurses and hospital staff began to notice and were cheering as well. I am pretty sure

I made a couple of jokes about how I may have a tumor in my hip, but it was not keeping me from dancing.

The next thing I knew, Summer was joking and saying that I should show Sara. I was not sure who Sara was, but Summer informed me that Sara was her boss. While I typically have an outgoing personality, Kativan holds back even less and instantly agreed. Next thing I knew, I was twerking in the oncology nursing director's office. Luckily for me, Sara thought my dancing was entertaining, and we formed a bond that day. Since then, Sara has stepped in many times to assist me through difficult obstacles and has requested that I be her patient when she occasionally works at the bedside. While I'm sure there's more to this memory that the drugs have erased, I cannot help but laugh and shake my head when I think about the day I twerked for the nursing director.

About this time, my smell sensitivity phase began. At first, soaps and laundry detergents were way too strong and easily made me nauseated. Every time I came to the hospital, there was a strange new scent that nauseated me there as well. Once noticed, I picked up on it everywhere: in the hall, the clinic rooms, the inpatient rooms, the teen rooms, and even outside on the playgrounds (although it was not as stout there).

Sometimes the scent would become too much, and I would have to step outside for fresh air. None of my family members or nurses could smell it, but we were aware of my smell sensitivity as a side effect of the chemo. Eventually, I noticed that it was coming from the area of my port, and it was determined that the cause was the sterile dressing bandaging my port needle.

At first, I tried to put a scented lotion on my skin near the dressing to mask the sour smell. I tried apple-scented lotion, but it only combined the two scents, making it worse. Mother tried getting several of the travel-size perfumes to spray around my hospital room, but half of those scents nauseated me, and the other half just mingled with the dressing's awful scent instead of masking it.

Finally, I shared my issue with my nurse, Cassie. She informed me that there are several different brands of dressings because many kids are allergic to Tegaderm, the type of dressing I had been using. While being nauseated by a scent is not an allergy, I was still able to try other dressings. Cassie brought in a sample of each dressing type and let me open each for a smell test. They were all so much better than the Tegaderm, and while I initially switched to a SorbaView dressing, I would eventually start using a Mepore dressing, which became my favorite due to its thinness, flexibility, light weight, and lack of scent. At some point, it was entered into the computer system at the hospital that I was allergic to Tegaderm. When asked about it, I never deny that I'm allergic.

Since then, I've even told pre-op that I am allergic to Tegaderm to prevent them from using it in the OR as well. I feel guilty about telling this little white lie, but it is so much easier than explaining how nauseous the scent of the Tegaderm makes me and hoping that whoever is placing the dressing listens and cares enough to actually use a different dressing, especially when it is being placed while I am sedated. While some of my favorite nurses are in on my little white lie, I suppose since I'm sharing it in this book, it will not be much of a secret anymore.

That isn't the only secret I've kept.

Initially, I was not going to be able to attend Junior Prom because I had chemo scheduled for that date. My friends were all aware that I wouldn't be able to make it and shared in my heartache. While pushing chemo out to a further date just because I wanted to was not an option, I learned that I could talk to my doctors if I had something important come up, like Junior Prom.

Luckily, Dr. Stine understood the importance and agreed it would be alright to postpone chemo a week so I could attend. He always emphasized quality of life. I found out last minute and ordered a dress online from Dillard's without even trying it on or seeing it in person because I could not risk going into a crowded store. While prom was also a risk because of the crowds, I got the approval from my doctor, so I decided it was a chance worth taking.

When I found out that I was going to be able to attend, I tweeted to let all of my friends know. Almost immediately, my good friend Matthew texted me and asked me to attend prom with him. I said yes, and we later planned for his bow tie to match my pale pink dress.

I did not see Matthew in person until the day of prom, so he was not able to do the ever-so-popular prom-posal. While a prom-posal was definitely not something that I expected, especially given the circumstances, Matthew still surprised me when he arrived to pick me up. Entering my house with a freshly-shaved head, he held a sign that read "Are you BALD enough to go to prom with me?" There was a circle cut out where Matthew stuck his bald head in to pose for photos. It was so thoughtful that he shaved his head for prom in honor of me, and it made for a great memory.

That night consisted of the usual prom schedule. First, a friend's house for group pictures. Next, to prom where we danced and snacked. Then, it was time for the after party. This is where my prom secret happened. Between prom and the after party, I stopped at my house to change out of my dress and into more comfortable clothes for the remainder of the night. It is no secret that many teens partake in drinking alcohol on prom night, but that was not an option for me while I was in treatment. I was aware of and content with my boundaries and wanted to attend for the social aspect.

My daily medicine routine included a dose of MiraLAX every night before bed. While the fact that I had to drink MiraLAX regularly for preventative reasons was not the most glamorous, it remained a fact. When I went home to change clothes, it was nearing time for my evening pills and MiraLAX. I preferred to mix it with apple juice, so while changing, I asked Mother to mix up my juice in a to-go cup. While I had either a water bottle or tumbler in mind, Mother mixed it in a red Solo cup instead.

As I was rushing out the door to go off with my friends, she handed me the red cup. All of my friends knew I was not partaking in any drinking, so throughout the early evening, several asked me what was in my cup. A few friends even jokingly accused me of trying to slip a beer, but I reassured them that it was just apple juice and even let them sniff my drink for confirmation.

What nobody knew was that while so many of my friends were partying and drinking, I was sitting with them throughout the night, sipping on MiraLAX. While I try to keep things as normal as possible despite treatment, this was one time that it was definitely not the same. Many of my friends had beer bottles and red Solo cups filled with liquor. Their perceptions were growing diluted. My red cup was filled with juice and medicine, and my fatigue was growing stronger.

19

During round five, I began struggling to make counts, and my chemo schedule had to be pushed out due to low blood levels. Because my levels were close, I only needed one additional week to recover. While I did make counts the following week, they were not high enough above the threshold to do chemo, meaning that they did not have as far to drop before I would need blood and platelet transfusions.

In round two, I had started getting blood and platelet transfusions and had received many by the time my count recovery was impacted. During rounds one morning, the doctor on call told my parents and me that I would need my first blood transfusion. My disgust with the thought of blood was initially so strong that I did not want to think about it or talk about it, and I definitely did not want to see it. I naively wished my parents would have suggested to the doctor that it be discussed in the hallway, but looking back, I know that would have been silly.

There was not much to discuss. I needed it.

Luckily, I was blessed with precious Rachael as my nurse for that first blood transfusion, which took a few hours. Rachael was close friends with my first nurse, Amber. Rachael gave me a dose of Ativan to make me sleepy and help calm my nerves, and then she waited until I fell asleep to bring in the blood bag. Once I'd drifted off, she tiptoed into my room and hung the blood on my IV pole with a pillowcase over it to keep me from seeing it if I woke up. This was just one of the many times she went out of her way to help me and make me more comfortable.

As I did more chemo, my bone marrow would grow weaker, causing me to need blood and platelet transfusions more often. A few months passed between that first transfusion and the first time I needed it while simultaneously getting chemo. I had become comfortable with the blood bags, and they no longer had to medicate me or wait until I was sleeping to transfuse.

A few days before the Sports Banquet, I was in the hospital for chemo and blood transfusions. I had to miss the graduation for the class ahead of me, and I was sad because many of my close friends were graduating. Maddi was able to FaceTime me from the audience, and I watched through my iPhone screen as several friends crossed the stage. I had received my chemo cocktail of strong medications that day, and my memory of watching the graduation is blurry. PaPaw sat with me in my hospital room while I watched. Eventually, Maddi had to mute her phone because I kept slurring words and the surrounding audience at graduation was hearing my medicated antics.

That same afternoon, I worked on a speech for the Sports Banquet, as Mrs. Renfrow had asked me to share a few words. I sat in my hospital bed and put pen to paper, using all of my medicated energy attempting to write a meaningful speech. I was discharged from the hospital the following day on a Sunday, and that following Tuesday was the Banquet.

On the day of the Sports Banquet, my friend Anna came over to my house after school to get ready. We helped each other with our makeup, and although all of my friends had seen me bald at that point, I decided to wear a short, brunette wig for fun. I chose a black jumpsuit that evening, but it was a little long for me, so I paired it with black high heels, and Anna wore a floral romper. We posed for several pictures before it was time to leave.

Daddy dropped Mother and me off at the door. As I was stepping out of the truck, I tripped and fell, landing on my knees. Mother was getting out of the front seat and immediately spun around to help me up. Blood and bits of asphalt encircled both kneecaps. A few nearby parents came running to help.

While a scraped knee is no big deal to a healthy person, it can be a big risk for an immunocompromised patient. We rushed into the elementary school building where the event was being held, and the elementary principal, Mr. Williams, escorted us to the nurse's office so we could get my knees cleaned and bandaged.

I instantly felt embarrassed that I'd fallen. I loved heels

so much and had more of that style shoe than any other. I didn't want anyone to think I didn't know how to walk in them. They probably knew, though, that I was just weak from the harsh treatments.

Because of the fall that night, I had to stop wearing heels until I could finish treatment and start physical therapy to regain my strength. I didn't even get to finish out the evening in my heels, as Mother made the smart decision to insist that I switch my black heels with her black sandals. While this fall would eventually cause me more trouble, it was settled for the evening.

I was still able to give my speech. When it was Mrs. Renfrow's turn to give out athletic awards to the cheerleaders, she called me to share a few words. I limped up to the stage and pulled out the speech I'd written a few days prior while medicated in the hospital. Just before beginning to read the speech to an audience full of classmates, teachers, coaches, families, and friends, I quickly realized that it was a hot mess. Luckily, I hadn't read anything aloud and was able to just wing it instead. The speech turned out great and from that point on, I would wing all of my speeches when asked to share my story, only bringing a notecard to write down a few numbers, facts, and statistics that I wanted to share.

When I finished, I was surprised with my own award: the Kaden Peebles True Scrapper Award. Mrs. Renfrow spoke about how courageous she believed I was and how I had persevered like a true Scrapper, the embodiment of our school's mascot. I was extremely honored and surprised to receive the award, and her heartfelt words were the icing on the cake. The fall and scraped knee were worth the evening.

The following morning, I went back to the hospital for my weekly clinic visit with my team. I showed the scraped knee to my nurse practitioner, Leslie, who examined it closely. She started me on an oral antibiotic but allowed me to go home and instructed me to call if anything changed or got worse. On Thursday, it was a little sore, but nothing I couldn't handle. On Friday, it was still sore, but again, not bad. I worked on a blog update and attended my little brother's baseball game. I drove myself, even though my right "driving knee" was the most sore and scraped of the two.

While driving home from the game, as I pushed my leg forward to step on the gas pedal, the soreness grew. When I got home, I decided to spend the rest of the evening resting in bed. Later that night, after everyone had gone to sleep, the soreness transitioned into pain. My phone battery had died, and my charger was in my car. I couldn't call my mom's phone in her bedroom to wake her, and she couldn't hear me hollering across the house over the television playing.

Alone in my room, I realized that since it hurt too much to walk, there was no other choice but to get on the floor and try to move myself. With my arms, I dragged my body across my bedroom, down the hall, and through the living room. Exhausted, I finally reached the house phone to call Mother. She helped me get back into my bed and retrieved some pain medication.

Throughout the night, the pain in my knee continued to build. Mother phoned the oncologist on call, who instructed us to drive to the ER at ACH. Mother and PaPaw took me, with Daddy soon following behind.

Once we arrived, the pediatric ER doctor examined my knee. The scrape appeared small, was not red, and had no pus. He examined to see if there was any kind of injury such as a torn ACL, but came up short. He was about to send me home when Mother requested he contact the oncologist on call who had instructed me to come to the ER. The oncologist was able to point out that because I had a low white blood cell count, I was prone to easily get infections, and that if an infection were to develop, we wouldn't see signs such as redness or pus because of the low count.

I was admitted to the oncology floor, and it was soon determined that I had cellulitis, an infection of the skin. Cellulitis is actually a common thing, but healthy people don't notice it because they have enough white blood cells to fight it off. I found humor in the diagnosis and joked about not wanting to post the name of the type of infection I had in a Facebook update because I didn't want any of my friends to confuse it with cellulite. There would be many laughs and jokes to come about my cellulitis, humor having become a way to cope with extreme stress.

I spent a few days in the hospital receiving strong IV antibiotics to help fight the infection and manage the pain. I wore a brace to support my still-swelling knee and help me limp to the bathroom. After a few days, the pain subsided, and I could walk again.

During the last day of that hospital stay, my nurse Rachael was in my room.

"I'm still surprised that a little scrape could cause such an infection," I shared with her.

"Isn't it amazing how incredible our white blood cells are? They are so smart that they can find infection in our bodies and so strong they can fight off infection. Our bodies know when we have an infection and need to produce more white blood cells," she said and explained to me that my white blood cells were not able to do their job because there were not enough of them after being wiped out by chemo. She knew of our shared faith and gave credit to God for designing our bodies so strong and so smart that when they are healthy, they can do wonderful things. Rachael's words and the soft tenor of her precious voice as she said them will always live in me.

Before long, it was summertime, and my siblings and friends were out of school. A couple weeks into the break, I reached the point in my treatment plan to discuss radiation.

ACH does not have oncology-radiation therapy on campus, but their sister hospital, University of Arkansas for Medical Sciences, does. I met with my radiation oncologist at UAMS, Dr. Penagaricano, who was able to evaluate me and determine my radiation plan with my primary oncologist, Dr. Stine.

During this seven-week period, I received 32 doses of radiation, once daily, Mondays through Fridays. Every couple of weeks, I would admit for chemo and ride in an ambulance between the two hospitals while also receiving chemo. Once you are inpatient, you cannot travel via private vehicles without being discharged, so the ambulance became my limo. My family rented an apartment in town, as our home in Nashville was over two hours away from Little Rock. My brother and sister joined my parents and me in a two-bedroom apartment for the summer. It was cozy, and we were in each other's spaces, but we enjoyed our time together, finding ways to entertain ourselves in a different city. Bre and I slept on twin beds in one bedroom and my parents took the second, while my brother slept on an air mattress in the living room. We would go to late-night movies when the crowds were thinner and get ice cream to beat the summer heat. PaPaw visited often, and he would sleep on the couch, stretching his long legs off the end. Maddi was even able to make surprise visits to help pass the time. We were all quite snug, but viewing it as a summer adventure made the hard times easier.

I was able to go home a couple of weekends during this period but had to remain nearby if I had chemo or my counts were dropping. I was at high risk for a fever, and a fever would equal an automatic hospital admission. So, I decided for the most part it was best to stay close to the hospital and not leave town.

Before it was time to begin receiving the radiation, my doctors discussed the option of having a surgery to move my ovaries, called an oophoropexy. This idea was presented as an option because the natural location of the ovaries can lead them to receive some scattered radiation and likely cause infertility issues. After lots of discussions with my doctors and parents, I decided this was a good decision to make for my reproductive health, and I was thankful I had the power to do so.

The surgery was outpatient and laparoscopic, so less invasive. The surgeon simply moved my right ovary farther to my right side and my left ovary close to the natural position of my right ovary. He used dissolvable stitches, so that over time and after the radiation was complete, the ovaries would come loose and naturally float back to their original position. The surgery was fairly simple, successful, and did not cause much pain. Thanks to good pain medications that first day, I mostly just felt excessive pressure in my stomach. I have a few dot-sized scars on my abdomen, and one is even hidden in my belly button.

Simple. Successful. Little Scarring. Yet at the age of 19, I would go into pre-menopause because of all the chemotherapy. My ovaries were failing, meaning I will likely have difficulties having children in the future. I didn't care about it then because I was far from wanting children, and I'm not too bothered by it now because I accepted it at such a young age. Adoption is always an option. As they say, it is what it is. Perhaps infertility is a small price to pay for survival.

22

One summer day, while I was receiving radiation and my mom was waiting for my treatment to end, she saw a girl playing in the waiting area. When the girl was called back for her radiation, our moms began chatting.

Mother learned that the girl's name was Asher Ray. She was six years old and, like me, had Ewing's Sarcoma. As they talked, Mother asked the girl's mom, Susan, where Asher's Ewing's was located. Mother often recalls how Susan shrugged it off, responding, "Oh, it's everywhere."

From day one, we always knew that my diagnosis could be worse, but this was the first time that Mother saw how much worse it could be.

A few days later in the pediatric oncology clinic, I heard this soft little voice in the clinic room next to mine. Asher was negotiating with her mom over a toy from the gift shop. In awe, I listened to her tiny voice saying exactly what she wanted with confidence. I could not help myself in wanting to connect a face to the voice, and I rounded the corner.

Entering her clinic room, I saw her itty-bitty body standing near the doorway. Despite her size, I quickly noticed that her bold spirit captured the entire room. I'd heard her parents call her by the nickname "Bit," and it suited her well.

Asher and I instantly formed a bond. We were both being treated by Dr. Stine, so we shared similar schedules. We saw each other often, both in the pediatric clinic for chemo and blood transfusions and in radiation treatment. Asher had done the traditional treatment for Ewing's Sarcoma, reached remission, relapsed, and started a new treatment. She lived in town and would often spend her mornings at school and her afternoons getting chemo or blood at the hospital. We spent many hours playing with Barbies, painting nails, scheming in the toy closet, petting therapy dogs, and playing games with our child life specialist, Keelen. Although she was 10 years younger, we were facing similar struggles, and she inspired me because she was a pro at the world that I was still learning to navigate. I was drawn to her old soul and personality, which resembled a younger version of myself.

Asher taught me that although you are supposed to wear a hospital band, sometimes you can just tape it to your IV pole and move on. She taught me how to have a good time in the hospital during long hours. She asserted we were part of the "scar club" and even once asked Maddi where *her* scar was located, assuming everyone has a scar. Maddi happened to have a small scar to share with Asher, and although I had not had any tumor removal surgeries, I had a small port scar and a few little scars from my oophoropexy. Asher declared us all members of the scar club, as she had many scars, including one down the full length of her thigh from a tumor resection surgery.

Asher also showed me the thrill of decorating my hospital room. Although she was doing most of her treatment outpatient at the time, she had made a cheerful habit of decorating when admitted to the hospital, and she passed it on to me.

In various hospital rooms, I've had Christmas trees, Thanksgiving pumpkins, banners, and signs. I often used battery-operated string lights and hung my Beads of Courage on my IV pole. For longer stays, I even brought home decor previously used in dorms and apartments. I would almost always have some sort of sign on my door and maybe even some window clings. Nurses, patients, and friends who have visited my hospital rooms over the years have given so many compliments. If it were not for Asher's inspiration, I would have never gone further than just bringing my own pillows and blankets to the hospital, never starting the decorating tradition that provided so much joy.

I know Asher had many days when she did not feel well or was in pain, but she didn't let that hold her back. She taught me how to fight cancer, and how to do it in a stylish outfit.

23

When I think of being in the hospital for many days at a time during that summer, I remember the warm scent of roasted coffee. Whoever was spending the night with me would start the day off with coffee, it would be sipped on throughout the day by all of the adults, and they would continue to drink it until bedtime. During rough nights when we were up during odd hours because of complications, my parents would continue to sip coffee. Perhaps they drank it around the clock for its flavor, or for its warmth to combat my 67 degree hospital room, or for the caffeine perks during irregular sleep schedules. Whatever the reason, my parents sipped it around the clock during hospital stays.

There was a coffee maker in the family house on our unit, so their Styrofoam cups remained full. I have heard other parents complain about the quality of the hospital coffee, and I am not sure that my parents thought it was the best, but they liked it enough and needed it enough to get through the long days. Occasionally, the smell would be too strong and make me sick, but usually it was comforting. As strange as it is for a teenager, sometimes when I was feeling crummy, I would ask my mom to let me smell her cup of coffee, as it made me feel warm and cozy.

One summer morning, I noticed several photos in my camera roll that I hadn't taken. My nurses working night shift had decided to take a bunch of goofy selfies for me to wake up and find. I scrolled through and saw pictures of Brian, Kelsey, and Ash-Leigh doing cheerful poses and Jennifer and Lindsey holding a sign that read "Good Morning Beautiful!" The best pictures were the ones of all five of the nurses attempting to build a pyramid. My nurses were always doing things like this that made my day.

That 4th of July was spent in the hospital. My siblings and I joined other patients from other units in the big hospital playroom, Camp Wannaplay, for some patriotic crafts, games, and snacks.

When it got dark, we all went upstairs to the basketball court on the hospital's roof to see the fireworks being shot from the Arkansas State Capitol across the interstate. Too weak to walk, I rode in a wheelchair. Still, I felt excited. We lined the court and looked to the sky as we waited for the display. My parents flashed pictures of my siblings and me grinning as we watched the fireworks in celebration of our country.

That summer was full of treatment that passed quickly because of all the good times we had along the way. Many days I was sick or not feeling well, but I got through it. The combination of chemo and radiation meant I had not one but two types of treatment causing my blood levels to drop low. I spent a lot of time getting blood and platelet transfusions.

This was when I learned to predict when my counts were dropping and if I would need a blood or platelet transfusion. I learned to predict my hemoglobin level, and if it is low, my guess is usually within half a unit of where my level actually is. The ability to know my body well enough to understand what was happening before any testing was an acquired skill. I can gauge it based on symptoms and how bad they are. A headache that starts in the back of my head when my hemoglobin drops below 10 is usually the first sign, along with fatigue. For context, anything below 10 or 11 is low, 7 feels really crummy, and a 6 is scary and dangerous. The drop feels like a pressure headache, but no pain medicine will help because it is due to a lack of oxygen flow. The lower the hemoglobin, the harder the headache, and it will sometimes wrap around the sides of my head. Another symptom is that my mood drops. As much as I wish I were not like this, I usually begin to get grumpy or irritable. Things bother me more easily, and this is a signal to my family. Sometimes, when my hemoglobin is below 7 or 6, I have additional symptoms like labored breathing and may require an oxygen cannula until we can get my blood levels higher. The treatment usually makes me toasty with hot flashes, but it is the exact opposite when I am low on blood.

That summer, I grew so cold that I wanted to wear a sweatsuit in the middle of July. Being away from home, I had not packed any sweats for the apartment. Mother searched everywhere and was finally able to find a black sweatsuit at Nike. I practically lived in that thick black sweatsuit throughout the heat of summer, just trying to get warm. I would wear it to radiation and while bundling under blankets in the apartment, although everyone else was in shorts trying to beat the heat.

During this time, I also learned how to tell if my platelets were low enough for a transfusion. This is much more difficult than the hemoglobin to interpret and something many patients cannot do. I can even determine when they are low, but not low enough to transfuse. Platelets stop bleeding and bruising, so blood and bruises are my indicators. Bruises happen to everyone, but several dark bruises of unknown origin are a sign. Blood when brushing or flossing teeth or blowing your nose is a sign, and nosebleeds that will not stop or have big clots mean extremely low platelets. All of these symptoms are common together and are usually paired with low hemoglobin. As the years have gone by, the combination of these symptoms has clued me in that something was wrong and led me to get unscheduled lab work. I have a pretty good track record and have never been wrong about counts, plus it has sped up the process of a couple of diagnoses and led to many unplanned transfusions that were much needed.

My advice to any cancer patient is to listen to your body. Only you know how you are feeling, and you have to recognize it so your doctors can help.

Most high school kids look forward to senior year. I was no different. When I was diagnosed with cancer, senior year became one big question mark. Would I be able to attend special senior events, would I get the classes I needed, and—the question I didn't want to think about but couldn't avoid—would I even graduate?

While I was not able to return to the classroom at the start of senior year, I was able to attend the traditional first-day-of-school Senior Breakfast. Maddi spent the night, and we both woke up early to get ready together. I was starving and we were running late, so I nibbled on a Pop-Tart during the short drive.

When we arrived, there was not enough time to sit down and eat. We spent most of our time socializing and taking pictures. During breakfast, I passed out Scrapper orange wristbands that read "Kaden's Courage" and "Psalm 112:7," my favorite Bible verse: "She does not fear bad news; she trusts confidently in the Lord to take care of her." Many of my classmates immediately began wearing their wristbands in my honor. My friend Leonard, the football team's quarterback, made a point to wear the wristband during every game. Even all these years later, he and several others still wear their wristbands daily. As the breakfast was ending, some friends offered to take the bracelets to school to pass out to others not at the breakfast.

Looking around the room, I took it all in. Being from a small town with only one school district, we had all grown up together. We had been in the classroom together from kindergarten on, and the majority of us went to the same district K through 12. We knew every face in the yearbook. I am not sure how many of us realized how special this bond was until we were older; I definitely did not until I spent nearly all of the second half of junior year homebound and received a taste of what it is like to not be in school.

Everyone was beginning to leave when I grabbed their attention with a, "Hey, real quick, everybody . . ." I wanted to take a minute to share an important message, and I wasn't going to let the chance pass me by.

As the chatter quieted and those standing near turned toward me, I said, "I know many of you are ready to be done with high school and reach graduation, but I've had the opportunity to see the world outside of high school early. I know it might be tempting to wish it away, but as somebody who has had it taken, please cherish every moment. This is our last year and then it's gone, so make the best of it." Some nodded in response, but I know that graduation still seemed so distant to many. Truthfully, I think most of them didn't know how to respond.

They all headed off to class, and I went home to rest. I spent the day napping in my bed and waiting for Maddi and my siblings to get out of school so that they could tell me all about their first day.

The next couple of weeks looked similar. On the days I was home and not at the hospital, I would rest during the day and wait for friends to come over after 3 p.m.

On Sundays, Maddi would routinely spend the night at my house. We'd watch *Keeping Up With The Kardashians* and drive through Sonic or McDonald's for fries or ice cream.

One Sunday in particular was different. Maddi came over earlier in the day with Hobby Lobby bags and a pair of jeans. We raided my mom's craft closet and began making Scrapper Jeans, a tradition of senior girls. We decorated jeans in our school colors to be worn on Fridays. By "we," I actually mean Mother and Maddi. I picked out the supplies I wanted to use on my jeans and told my mom how I'd like the designs, but with my blood levels being extremely low that day, my energy was also low. I rested on the couch while Maddi and my mom crafted. They worked well into the evening and stayed up late crafting until it was finally time to go to sleep. Scrapper jeans are known for being highly decorated, and the good ones take more than a day or two to make. The more detail the better. The goal is to make the jeans as elaborate as possible with paintings and patterned fabrics cut into letters to spell out your name, "senior," or "Scrappers." There are often ribbons, stones, and appliques. I wanted my jeans to be as flashy as possible.

Maddi spent the night with me and went to school that Monday morning. Not long after she left, I began to feel even more crummy. Mother came to check on me in bed and discovered I had a fever. Oncology patients have to watch closely for fevers. If they get higher than 101 degrees, it becomes necessary to go to an emergency department within half an hour. It's important to move quickly because antibiotics need to be started as soon as possible and lab cultures need to be drawn from a port or central line.

My fever was 101.4, so it was time to move.

Being over two hours from ACH, I would go to my local county hospital in these situations, where my grandpa, Sam, worked as one of the standing physicians. From there, we would start antibiotics, draw labs, and contact the oncologist on call at ACH. I would be transported via ambulance to ACH's ER, where they would admit me to 4K. Upon being admitted for a fever, there were two requirements in order to go home: being fever free for at least 48 hours and having negative lab cultures.

It took me a few days to achieve both requirements for that hospital stay, and after discharge I still was not feeling completely well. Mother had grabbed my Scrapper jeans and some supplies on our way out the door to the hospital and had spent the week sitting by my hospital bed, decorating my jeans. She even made a trip to the store for more craft supplies. All of my nurses and doctors had watched the jeans' transformation throughout the week as my mom worked her magic with paints, rhinestones, ribbons, and fabrics. Mother even painted a bald cheerleader in uniform, right down to the bow on her bald head.

Before long, it was Thursday, and we only had a little over 24 hours left until the first football game of the season. I was determined to make it to the first pep rally and game wearing my Scrapper jeans. With the help of my nurse practitioner, Katherine, we were able to convince my doctors to let me leave the hospital and attend the game the next day. They were hesitant because my counts were still low, and I was obviously not feeling my best, but they could see how much it meant for me to attend, and I had met the two initial requirements to go home.

The next day, I excitedly dressed in my Scrapper jeans with a matching T-shirt and a big orange bow. Since I was bald, I asked my mom to fasten one of my cheer bows on a baby headband so I could wear it while cheering on my team.

Against the odds, I arrived on The Hill.

It's an annual tradition for seniors to stand on the gym floor while the cheerleaders tumble and dance. One of the teachers grabbed a chair to roll onto the gym floor for me, so I wouldn't tire too much. While it was tough to see my teammates cheering without me, it was nice to be with them as we all shouted and clapped along. Soon, it was time for a special senior moment during one of the band dances. Each year, the girls line up in three rows according to their grade, with the senior girls in front. The cheerleaders yell "Beat those (opposing team's mascot), yay!" and the front row of senior cheerleaders hold hands and drop to their knees. As silly as it is, it's something only the senior girls get to do and a reward for cheering through senior year. I had watched the girls in the classes ahead of me have this and other special senior perks, and it burned to miss out on this senior reward. I teared up. It was also difficult to watch my sister cheer on the high school team and think of all the memories we were supposed to be making together that we wouldn't have. Still, it made me happy to watch her excel as the only sophomore in a stunt group of all seniors, and I was the proudest big sister.

After the pep rally, Maddi and I went to Walmart for spirit supplies for the game's student section, including confetti cannons and cowbells. We stopped at Sonic and then headed to my house so I could squeeze in a quick nap before the game.

I was able to stay for the whole game that night, alternating between the student section and sitting with my family. It was a big win that would be the start of an undefeated season. I was so proud of the boys in my class that I had grown up with, as well as my sister and the other cheerleaders. As usual, the boys worked hard and the girls cheered nonstop for hours with constant jumps, chants, stunts, tumbling, dances, and traditions. Being under the Friday night lights up on The Hill in Nashville is a feeling like none other, whether performing or observing from the crowd. The sense of unity and the spirit of our community is something I wish everyone in this world could experience at least once. I have been blessed to experience it on many Friday nights.

There would be Friday nights that season when I could only go for a portion of the game, and there would be Friday nights when I had to stream the game from home or the hospital. On the days that chemo came before football and I'd be at the hospital rather than on The Hill, I'd never forget to pack my Scrapper jeans.

Soon, I met a friend who was going through similar struggles. Solid with broad shoulders, Omari towered over me. Any stranger could clearly tell this guy was an athlete. Unfortunately, he was missing out on his junior year of football for the same reason I was missing my senior year of cheer. Omari was also fighting cancer. He had acute myeloid leukemia or AML. He went to school near the hospital, but because of treatment, we spent countless Fridays in the hospital together talking about how much we wished we were doing our favorite sports. On Saturday mornings, we'd ask how each other's teams had done the previous night. Omari would go on to beat leukemia, return to school, and play his senior year—an inspiration to countless others. We are still close today and try to catch up with each other every so often. We have both been through a lot these last few years but have managed to keep surviving and overcoming. Surrounding yourself with people like Omari makes it easier to persevere.

25

At Nashville High School, homecoming is reserved for seniors only. There is no dance, just a day of traditional celebrations and activities for the homecoming court. Twelve senior girls are nominated. The football players vote for seven of them: five football maids, one maid of honor, and one queen. The following day, the senior class votes for five class maids.

The voting is usually held on a Monday and Tuesday a few weeks prior to homecoming. Sometimes it can be easily predicted when it will be held but not always. The voting is not announced ahead of time, but is done at the end of the day during football practice, so word travels fast. Prior to my senior year, I watched girls cry on the bathroom floor and sisters hope that both would make it. Every girl wanted to have a special day and wear a pretty dress. Every girl secretly (or not-so-secretly) hoped that she'd be picked.

My senior-year homecoming voting experience went a

little differently from most. Instead of being at school during the voting, I was home. Bre was at cheer practice. Knowing the voting was starting that day, Bre texted our mom, who made sure not to tell me. I was awaiting the results of my first set of important scans two days later, and Bre and my mom didn't want to give me any more unnecessary stress by making me aware of the voting. I never said it aloud because I knew I had more serious concerns, but I wondered if not being around and in class every day would make it even more unlikely that I'd be voted in.

I was sitting on my bedroom couch trying to do some online schoolwork, but mostly online shopping, when Mother came into my room and sat next to me.

Thanks to word of mouth, Mother had gotten news of the votes a few minutes prior to the announcement. During the few minutes after voting and before homecoming court was announced, one of the football players sent a text to my friend Anna with the results. Anna was with my sister in the cheer room and shared the results with her, and then Bre texted my mom. My mom had come into my bedroom so she could be there when my sister and Anna called to tell me once the announcement was made on the speaker. It seemed odd that Anna was calling my mom, but as soon as I answered the phone, she and Bre excitedly informed me that I had been voted onto the homecoming court as maid of honor.

I was surprised to learn that I'd made it. Although it will not be landing me a job or getting me into Heaven, it was still special to me because it showed me that even though I was not going to school every day, my friends still thought of me. To this day, I know that if I were in trouble or needed something, I could go to many of the guys who played football in my class and they would do anything to help me. That is true friendship.

As soon as my sister got out of cheer practice the next day, Mother drove us to Little Rock for my doctor's appointment. Once in Little Rock, we made the impulsive decision to go dress shopping. I wanted to find my dress fast. Our school's tradition is that the queen wears a white dress and all of the other girls can wear any color. I was the maid of honor, so any color was an option. With eleven girls picking, some would likely make the same choice. If I found my dress quickly, my hope was nobody else would wear the same color.

While I am a pink girl through and through, we entertained the idea of other colors. We discussed red, my signature color because it looks best on me. We also played with the idea of green—opposite red on the color wheel, meaning it also goes well with my coloring. Ultimately though, we decided on my favorite: pink. I can't think of a time in my life when pink was *not* my favorite color or a time when I did not have a pink bedroom. Mother chose red, blue, and yellow for my nursery, but that would not have been my choice.

I almost always choose to wear pink or black, the most flattering color, for everything from day-to-day clothes to more formal outfits. So, it was no surprise when I chose a hot pink ball gown.

The dress was gorgeous, but my crafty mom did a little work to make it even more perfect. The bodice was covered in rhinestones, but she was able to add more stones in the few spots that did not have any. We also searched in several stores to find the biggest hoop skirt possible to make the skirt extra poofy. Since I was bald and would not be getting my hair fixed, we decided to make a little extra something for me to wear on my head. While we discussed a wig, I ultimately decided not to wear one, because it did not feel like me. Instead, my mom dyed a white lace headband to match my dress and added jewels to it as well. The queen traditionally wears a crown, and I did not want to take away from my friend Alexus, who would be crowned queen, but she liked my headband and encouraged me to wear it on my bald head.

26

The following morning, I woke early in our Little Rock apartment to shocking news. My first friend at the hospital, Taylor, the boy who always assigned songs to different chemotherapies and put on sock puppet shows for nurses, had died during the wee hours of the morning. I was friends with his mother, Angela, on Facebook and saw that someone had tagged her in a post, sending their condolences.

I suppose that as I made friends with others in cancer treatment, I was aware of the possibility they could die, but before that moment, I had not experienced it firsthand. The news came as even more of a shock because Taylor was in remission and had finished treatment six months before. The cause of his death was not cancer, but heart failure caused by his treatment. Whereas most chemotherapy drugs are clear, Taylor's chemotherapy drug, Doxorubicin, better known as the "red devil" after its red coloring, is what caused his heart failure. This was a chemo that we both had taken, and I was scheduled to start another round of it that day.

Taylor's mom had warned me before a prior round how nauseated it would make me and how terrible the vomiting would be. It has even made me violently vomit popcorn through my nose. It is an extremely harsh chemo, one of the harshest I have ever had, but it takes something awful to kill something as awful as cancer. In Taylor's case though, it had done more than kill his cancer.

The reality of death and long-term side effects in the cancer world were suddenly painfully clear. With each chemo, I have to sign forms indicating that I am aware of all possible side effects. The side effects are broken down into how frequently they occur. Heart failure is listed, along with many other awful side effects, but it is not at the top of the list. Taylor's heart failure showed me that just because a side effect is not super common does not mean it cannot happen or that it will not happen. Suddenly, every possible side effect seemed like a threat.

With the terrible news, we went to clinic, where the emotional rollercoaster continued. The nurses are not allowed to disclose any patient information due to HIPAA, but they can mourn lost patients with other patients if a patient brings it up and makes it clear they are already aware. Pediatric oncology units are different from most units, where patients are in and out for one-time visits. The patients spend so much time together that they begin to know each other and become friends. It was clear that some of the nurses in clinic were sad that morning because of Taylor's death, despite the smiles they tried to press on their faces as they kept working.

I was talking about how sad and shocked I was with one of Taylor's and my favorite nurses when she quietly asked if I had talked to our other friend that day. She casually mentioned that nurses are not allowed to tell patients anything about other patients and said, "There may be someone who is friends with Taylor but is not aware." I read between the lines and realized she was telling me that Faijon did not know about Taylor, and none of the staff could tell him.

A little unsure of myself, I asked, "Should I go and talk to Faijon?" She simply winked. I knew that Faijon came to clinic every Wednesday to be examined or admitted for chemo. I also knew that the hallways have screens with patient initials and clinic room numbers.

I found Faijon's room and knocked on the door, questioning how I was going to do this.

"Come in," I heard his soft voice say.

When I entered, Faijon was alone in the room, hooked up to an IV pole with fluids, prepping for chemo. He was sitting on the bench provided for family members, so I took a seat on his patient exam table. "Well, how are you?" I asked, trying to make conversation.

Not usually a guy of many words, Faijon nodded and quipped, "Doing good, you?"

I didn't have it in me to keep up the small talk any longer and quickly blurted out, "I have bad news . . ." He shot me a confused look and nodded his head for me to continue. After an awkward pause, I continued, "Taylor hasn't been doing well. He was having heart problems, and it got bad." I paused to think, realizing bad didn't explain how bad. "He died this morning."

Faijon's face dropped. I held my breath while waiting for his response.

"I saw Taylor about a week or so ago. He was getting follow-up scans." Faijon shook his head. "He looked so frail. My mom had even noticed that he looked like he was doing worse than me. It seemed weird because he isn't doing chemo anymore, and I still am."

We sat in silence. I thought about how little sense it all made.

I think we were both unsure of what to say. We talked about how we would miss him, but we were mostly shell-shocked. The air felt thick, the discussion having brought our own mortality to the table.

It wasn't long before a nurse knocked on the door looking for me. She said Dr. Stine was waiting for me in my clinic room.

When I returned, Dr. Stine shared two things. First, my counts were too low for chemo that day, and we were postponing the red devil until the following week. This was a relief. After all, the red devil had killed my friend. It had killed my friend. I would go on to take it the following week and many more times, but the day's events encouraged me to always ask for extra echoes to examine my heart and make sure it was doing alright.

The second topic that Dr. Stine wanted to discuss was my scans from the week before, the first scans post-radiation. We were really hoping the tumor would be dead or smaller at the very least.

Dr. Stine pulled up the imaging of my pelvis to show me. He spoke slowly and confidently. "Kaden, it shows the radiation worked." His grin reinforced his words. This was good. Very good. I had reached remission. I was cancer free!

October 7th will forever be marked in my mind. All in one day, I had learned that Taylor died, broken the news to Faijon, been told by Dr. Stine that I had reached remission, failed to make counts, and headed home. This was also two days after making homecoming. I'm sure that my mind was in a different place from the other girls on the homecoming court. This series of events taught me the true meaning of priorities. While homecoming was important to me and would have been top priority had the situation not been what it was, beating cancer and losing a friend was higher on my list of what mattered.

The radiation killed the tumor, but I never had surgery to remove it. So, my left iliac wing holds a dead tumor. Over time, the doctors said, my body should absorb it. I am not sure if the tumor has yet been fully absorbed, as I have stopped requesting to see my semi-annual scans and simply accept verbal results, but I know it was there for a while after I reached remission because radiology techs would see it and do additional imaging.

To me, the tumor never felt like a foreign object, although I can understand why others would view it that way. I viewed the tumor as part of me . . . just a little extra, a bonus part that represents the inner battle I waged, both physically and mentally. Fighting cancer felt like fighting myself.

27

At home, Maddi was planning a surprise party. She had contacted my family, and PaPaw was helping her set up. She somehow
managed to invite a large group of my friends and classmates,
decorate, and get food in less than two hours. She and PaPaw
had everyone park behind my house so I wouldn't see any cars.

When I was getting out of the car, I saw an unfamiliar
truck pulling into the driveway. I asked aloud who it was, and
my mom and sister just brushed it off and ushered me toward
the door.

As I opened the door and stepped into the family room,
I was shocked to see the room crowded full of friends yelling,
"Surprise!" and tossing balloons. Tears of pure joy to be living
this moment spilled over my cheeks and trickled onto my pink
top.

Over the next few weeks, while the other girls were preparing for homecoming, I was preparing a eulogy for Taylor's service. His mom, Angela, had asked me to speak along with two of our nurses, Rachael and Amber. I had spoken in public several times before but never at a funeral service. I wanted to share some of my favorite memories of Taylor but was unsure of the best and most appropriate way to do so. Rachael and Amber gave me some tips, as did Mother, who helped me choose the right wording. I never imagined that at age 17 I would be speaking at a friend's funeral.

I had not been to many funeral services before this and was unsure of what to expect. Several of my nurses gathered in the hall beforehand, and we made small talk. Besides my nurses and child life specialist, most of the faces in the pews were unfamiliar. When it was time to speak, Rachael, Amber, and I made our way to the front of the room. We stood together and took turns sharing memories of our times with Taylor. They each held one of my hands when it was my turn to speak, and we all supported each other during a difficult moment. I later debated if I should have said this or that differently or included something not mentioned, but I think that if Taylor were there, he would have been proud that I stood up and spoke. Taylor was an easygoing guy, and I always admired that about him. He never seemed to let anything get to him, a quality we should all strive toward.

The following week, I returned to ACH for the same chemo that put Taylor into heart failure. Despite being in remission, I still had to finish chemotherapy because the treatment plan is intended to be carried out completely. The idea is that if there are any micro cancer cells in your body, the remaining treatment will get them. This is similar to how you have to continue taking an antibiotic even if you start to feel better.

I never had any hesitation in doing the chemo, as it was my only chance to survive, to live. But Taylor's death did make me a little nervous about that round. I received it three days in a row, and when it was time for the first dose of the round, my nurse and friend Lauren B. happened to be on the unit. She wasn't working that shift but had come by to drop something off. She stopped in my room right as my nurse was hanging the chemo on my IV pole. I told Lauren B. of my worries, and she immediately offered to stay with me during the infusion. She sat on my hospital bed for the next hour. We talked about Taylor and about other things, just to keep my mind off the chemo. It meant a lot to me that she would take the time to sit with me when she wasn't on the clock. I was medicated that evening, so what exactly we discussed is a blur, but her thoughtful act stayed in my memory.

After chemo, homecoming preparations continued. Wednesday of homecoming week was eventful and fast-paced. It was Mother's birthday, I had an appointment at ACH for chemo and blood transfusions, and that evening was the traditional homecoming parade. I spent the morning and early afternoon resting in clinic while tanking up on blood and continuing my treatment plan with chemo infusions. As soon as I was done at the hospital, my parents rushed me back home to make it in time for the parade.

Exhausted from the long clinic day, I napped the entire drive home. Ironically, my friend DeaAnn was also rushing back from ACH to Nashville. She was a member of Circle of Friends, the fundraising chapter for ACH and had a meeting there that morning. She had also graciously offered to drive me in her car in the parade, which was the start of our budding friendship.

By parade time, I was low on blood and achy from chemo, but I did not want to miss the parade for the world. I sat on the top back part of DeaAnn's red convertible between my two escorts, Trey and Billy. DeaAnn drove and Andrew sat in the front passenger seat next to her. We held custom footballs monogrammed with our names that read "Homecoming 2015." I put on my best smile and did what any crowd-lover would do: waved big and tossed goodies to the lines of people on the sidewalks as we rode through town.

Maddi and I joined our families for dinner, and from there I went straight to bed. I was absolutely zonked but proud to have been able to push through and participate.

Two days later, it was time for the main homecoming activities. That morning, Maddi and Jessica came over to my house for breakfast before we went to do our makeup and they went to their hair appointments. Going bald, I was saving time not having to do the latter.

After lunch and an hour of standing and smiling for pictures, I grew weak and rested in the locker room. While sitting next to my mom and sister, I became queasy. Mother quickly grabbed a blue bag in case I got sick, and Bre searched for a Sprite. I was hot in my ball gown, and they were both fanning me. Maddi and our friend Alexus sat nearby for support. I was able to hold back any major vomiting, only getting a little sick and mostly dry heaving. We later laughed about it, because nobody in the ceremony crowd had any idea that I'd been doubled over earlier that same hour. I put on my big girl face and smiled from ear to ear as I walked the homecoming court. It took me back to my little girl pageant years, as I made sure to look directly into the crowd and pose. The lights shimmered above, and I saw smiling faces in every direction. I thrived being in the spotlight, and moments like this continually inspired me to keep pushing through the tough times.

After the ceremony, I stayed for a few pictures but left early enough to squeeze in a nap before the next ceremony at the football game. We had a disguised blessing that night: rain. Nobody wants rain on homecoming. It is just not ideal to have hair and makeup and pretty gowns in pouring rain on a muddy football field. It worked well for me though, because instead of walking across the football field with our fathers, we walked down the track. While the football field was more exciting, the walk would have been longer and more difficult for me. As it was, Daddy had to provide a lot of support, his strong right arm under my left keeping me steady. He wore a fedora, and I wore a black fur hat—needed by both of us to keep our bald heads warm. I'll always treasure that feeling of him walking next to me.

We all sat under a tent on one end of the track, right next to the field. It was special because tradition is for the homecoming girls to stand next to the cheerleaders for some of the chants and lead the crowd. I was elated to be back under the Friday night lights. And, I was able to cheer next to my sister. While I was robbed of my senior cheer season, moments like this made it easier.

28

One of the absolute best things to come from getting cancer
was Keagan Provost. I met Keagan when he was 5 years old.
First I met his mom, Robin, in the hallways of 4K. The morning I met Robin, I had a clinic appointment and had stepped
upstairs to say hi to one of my favorite nurses. She introduced
us. I first noticed Robin's blue hair, then her laundry basket.
Her arms were covered in tattoos, and she had many piercings.
She seemed at home in the hospital, carrying her laundry to the
family room. I wondered about this pretty lady and her story.
Not long after that, we became Facebook friends. I'm not sure
who sent a friend request, but I learned that her son was Keagan and that he had brain cancer—Ependymoma.

About a week later, I was admitted to 4K for a week of
chemo. As soon as I got to the floor, Robin knocked on my hospital room door. She said, "I saw you through the window with
your big floppy hat and cheetah-print dress! Want to come by

Keagan's room to meet him?"

As I entered Keagan's room, his big warm eyes felt welcoming to me. I sat at the end of his bed. A yellow liquid-filled tube taped to his nose funneled inside his right nostril. His IV pump had bags hanging on every hook.

Robin was introducing me as I took in how sick he appeared. "This is Kaden! She's here to hang out. Can you tell her hi?"

"Hiiii!" he said with genuine enthusiasm. "Do you wanna watch *Cars*?"

"Sure!" I said, smiling.

Robin plumped a pillow next to Keagan, saying, "You can lie down if you want to rest."

I leaned back and noticed his scalp was covered in scars. I would later learn they were from over 40 brain surgeries. His body told a story of the years of treatment he had endured. It was apparent that this kid was strong and not just because he had cancer.

From that first moment, he let me into his world without question, which made our bond grow. Right away, Keagan acted as if he had known me his whole life and treated me like his best friend. Despite our age differences, we understood each other because our struggles were similar.

Keagan got his strength from his momma. As I spent time with her, I learned that she has several tattoos in memory of kids she has bonded with who have had cancer and died. Also, every month she lets a kid with cancer pick the color of her hair. She began to dye her hair because Keagan was upset about having to be bald for chemo and brain surgeries. She did it as a distraction, so strangers would stare at her instead of making Keagan uncomfortable by staring at him.

Robin, Keagan's dad Mike, his little brother Jaxon, and I would become so close that they called me their daughter-in-law, and I called them my in-laws, an inside joke referencing what happened in the hospital one night.

It had been a long day, and we were all feeling sad. Keagan had received bad scan results again, I was sick from chemo, and I was missing Senior Cheer Night. While my sister and brother graciously stepped in for me at the football game so I could still be recognized even though I couldn't make it in person, I was feeling some serious FOMO from being in the hospital instead. I had been on my chemo cocktail of Benadryl, Ativan, and Phenergan around the clock for about 48 hours.

It was nearing midnight, and we were all desperate for something to cheer us up. I suggested the idea to Robin as something silly to do, and from there, she and our nurses ran with it. Keagan and I were going to have a wedding in the hospital.

I didn't have anything white in my suitcase, so Robin loaned me a white cardigan to wear over my blue silk pajamas, and she made my bridal veil from toilet paper. Keagan wore a top hat made from construction paper. The nurses decorated the hall and made tissue flower bouquets. Robin walked to the cafeteria and got us cake to eat after the ceremony. Our nurse,

Matt, was the officiant. He wrote up vows for us to both promise to keep fighting and to beat childhood cancer. When he spoke, he pretended to have a thick Southern-meets-British accent, which left everyone in giggles.

It was Daddy's turn to stay with me that night, one of the first nights that my parents swapped off instead of both staying. He walked me down the aisle, or rather the hospital hallway. The nurses had decorated their work station as an altar, where I met Keagan, getting down on both knees so that I could be closer to his six-year-old height. The nurses had asked us both to select a song, mine for before the ceremony and his for after. I could hear my song of choice, "Fight Song" by Rachel Platten, playing in the background.

The whole ceremony is a blur, but I remember how excited Keagan was for the cake. When it was over, we both took off walking in the wrong direction, neither of us holding our IV poles. Luckily, our parents were right behind us and were there to push the poles. We were too busy dancing to Keagan's song choice, "Uptown Funk" by Bruno Mars, to realize we were walking away from the direction of the family room where we planned to celebrate, but once we got turned around, we were able to go enjoy the cake. I can't hear that song without thinking of Keagan and his love of it, along with everyone's laughter because he could never quite enunciate the "n" as he sang "uptown funk you up."

By the time I returned to my hospital room and settled in bed, it was nearing 2 a.m., and I decided to call Mother. When she answered the phone, I excitedly informed her that I had gotten married. She knew that I was in the hospital getting chemo and was heavily medicated, but she played along until she realized I was serious. The following day, she asked Keagan and me about our wedding, and he kept telling her the best part was that we ate cake afterward and how he wore a cool hat. From that point on, we referred to each other as husband and wife, and I was often recognized as Keagan's wife throughout the hospital.

Keagan and I spent many long hours in the hospital together over several years. We have eaten many grilled cheese sandwiches with the "cheese on the bottom," as he preferred to call what was really just a regular grilled cheese. We've spent many afternoons with one of us sitting in the hallway of the other's hospital room because the one inside the room had caught a contagious bug. We've done several local interviews together. Others are always amazed at our story, how different we are, yet how strong our bond—how we came together because we were fighting the same evil.

Once we were doing a local news interview that was being filmed live. It was an advertisement for a fundraising event for the oncology unit at ACH, and there were several superheroes there to promote the event. Because it was 5 a.m., one of the superheroes was holding Keagan next to me as he slept. When the segment was over and the superhero handed Keagan back to Robin, she realized that the whole time we were filming and thought he was sleeping, he was silently seizing. Luckily, one of our nurses was present for the interview and was able to start taking care of Keagan. They immediately rushed him to the ER. We thought we might lose him.

There were many days that Keagan defied obstacles and countless doctors' predictions. It seemed like he was constantly getting bad news, yet he continued to overcome and thrive.

29

Fall is my favorite season for many reasons. I love how the air cools and the leaves change. I love that school starts back and it's time to open fresh notebooks and plan for the year ahead. There is a sense of excitement for the holidays on the horizon and the football games starting up.

One Friday evening after taking the red devil, I was discharged from the hospital. I had plans to attend the game, despite just spending three days infusing one of the toughest chemos.

I continued the cocktail of drugs to fight the nausea, packed blue bags, bundled up, and headed for the stands with my family. I spent the first half of the game watching and cheering with my family while my sister cheered in uniform from the sidelines. Around halftime, exhaustion swept over me. I decided to go home and rest. I told Mother that I was going to walk down to the track to say goodbye to Bre before I left.

Someone suggested that I do a cheer with my fellow cheerleaders. I thought it would be fun, and they quickly made space for me in the line. What started out as just one cheer turned into cheering the entire second half of the game. I only did chants with motions, as my body was far too weak and out of practice to do any jumping or tumbling. When the girls performed band dances, I stood offside the track cheering for them. Before getting sick, I would have thought that doing chants alone would be boring, but that night I had a blast. This is not to say it was not challenging and that it did not drain me for the entire weekend, but it was all worth it. It was the best night of my senior year, and I loved getting to cheer alongside my sister.

It wasn't long before Halloween rolled around. I began brainstorming for a unique costume. When you spend enough time in the world of cancer, you start to get a bit of a warped sense of humor. Being my first—and what I thought would be my only—Halloween bald, I decided I wanted to dress up as a bald character. This is how I came to pick Uncle Fester from the TV show *The Addams Family*.

My brother had a black cape from an old Darth Vader costume. All I needed was a lightbulb and some dark undereye makeup. Mother ordered a costume light bulb that would be safe to hold in my mouth, and we put a glow stick inside. At my grandparents' house, I sat on the front porch with the fake, glowing lightbulb in my mouth and a big bowl of candy in my lap. I think it confused some of the younger children, as one girl asked, "Are you a boy or a girl?" I think she could tell that I'm a girl, but the male costume had her puzzled. I found her curiosity comical. Parents loved my costume, instantly recognizing the character.

After passing out candy, still in my Uncle Fester costume, Daddy and I ran into Walmart to grab a few things. Fatigued, I rode the automatic scooter that the store provides. Rolling down the aisles, I met many other customers. Daddy describes how entertaining it was to watch passersby initially laugh at my costume, then feel guilty for laughing at a kid with cancer. Their faces would go from glee to guilt. I was not offended by any laughter, as it was a joke I'd purposefully created to make light of something dark, but it was kind that others were trying to be considerate.

The Scrappers had not lost any games and were headed to the 4A state football finals. Being undefeated is always worth bragging about, but it called for even more bragging that year—our first year with a new coach. The combination of a stellar new coach and an excess of talent was the winning formula.

The State Championship Game was held in Little Rock, where ACH is located. I had appointments that week, so Mother and I were in town during the days leading up to the big game. Daddy and my siblings joined us that day. We all loaded up in my mom's Tahoe and braved the bumper-to-bumper traffic and long lines outside of the stadium. There were so many familiar faces that night, I would have been surprised to find anyone left in Nashville. We arrived early enough to find good seats only a few rows up from the field. My sister was on the sidelines cheering, and everyone in the stands was on their feet. My science teacher, Mr. Horne, and his family sat behind us, and he provided excellent commentary throughout the game's stomach-dropping ups and downs. In the end, our Scrappers went undefeated and won the state championship!

The excitement was contagious despite the stadium's security guards who played by their own rules. We had been warned how strict they'd be, and the warning was no exaggeration. They had rules as to who could go onto the football field after the game, which did not include just any fan. It did include cheerleaders, but despite being in my official uniform warm-ups and on the roster list, security was not letting me onto the field after the game because I was not already on it. They did not seem to understand that I was not active due to my health.

Luckily, a friend who works for the school district who was already on the field caught wind that I was not being allowed to go. She secretly slipped her pass to my friend Joel who ran the pass over to the sidelines and handed it to our friend Trey's mother, who brought it to me in the stands. This coordinated, baton-passing situation was such a generous gesture, making it possible for me to head down to the field to see my friends who had just cheered and played.

Several photos were taken as my eyes filled with tears. I was proud of my friends who had worked so hard. Some of the boys had already made their way into the locker room as the celebration continued. Hunter and Leonard noticed that I had missed the opportunity to see several of the players, so they asked me if I would like to join them in the locker room to celebrate. Leonard ran ahead to make sure everyone was still dressed, and Hunter stayed with me. My feet pounded forward as hard as I could run across the field to reach the locker room. Hunter moved at the same pace by simply speed walking. He must have been able to tell how tired my body was, and he kept patting me on the shoulder, encouraging me with every step.

When we arrived at the locker room, the music was pumping and the guys were cheering. Each step I took was more like a mini leap with my hands clapping above my head. We all formed a circle and danced in celebration. After a few songs, I told the team how proud I was of them and congratulated them on their big win before leaving the locker room.

My phone was dead, and my legs felt like Jell-O. I made my way to the parking lot with no clue where my family was or where our car was parked. It didn't take me long before seeing a group of friends from Nashville. They gave me somewhere to sit and rest while they called my family to come pick me up. When my family found out where I'd been, they couldn't help but laugh at how I was almost denied the opportunity to celebrate with my friends but ended up in the locker room with the team, having a dance party.

Senior year became more about the new opportunities presented to me rather than the lost ones. I spent a lot of time with
my child life specialist, Emily. She did a good job treating me
like an adult and providing activities that were age appropriate.
So often on the pediatric side, professionals don't know how to
talk or relate to teenagers.

Emily encouraged me to join the hospital's Youth Advisory Council, better known as YAC. YAC was made up of about
a dozen teenagers who met monthly with a child life specialist
named Amanda. Some months I would make the drive in for
the meeting and others I was already inpatient in the hospital.
On inpatient days, I would come in my loungewear, hooked up
to an IV pole with chemo pumping, often medicated. During
our meetings, we were asked for suggestions to improve the
hospital.

I silently wondered if any action would actually be taken to implement our suggestions, but I proceeded to give two. First, I wanted to improve the Wi-Fi, making it possible for patients to stream Netflix and YouTube. Second, I wanted the doors leading from the atrium outside the oncology unit to the elevator area to be handicap accessible. Many times, someone would be pushing me in a wheelchair toward the elevator, and it would require more than two hands to hold the door while pushing both the wheelchair and IV pole.

Amanda worked her magic and knew just who to connect with to make both of these suggestions possible. Now, every time I stream Netflix at the hospital or use those handicap doors, I am reminded of all that I learned and all those I met that year during YAC. This experience made me feel like my opinion actually mattered and that my advocacy could be taken seriously.

One of the perks of joining YAC was the volunteer badge that scored me access through several of the hospital entrances for staff and volunteers only. This made it much easier to walk to the clinic by shortening the distance dramatically. After several years of wearing the badge, the corners began to fray and the lamination started to lift from the paper. It was even pointed out to me that the hospital has changed logos and rebranded, meaning nobody even uses the same style badge anymore. Nonetheless, on hospital days, that badge is something I made sure to always have in my purse. It was a reminder of the many ways I can and should advocate, not only for myself, but for others as well.

While the hospital can be chaotic, some things are consistent. During treatment for Ewing's, two things always remained the same. Every time I went to the clinic, my port would be accessed, and after every round of chemo, protocol was to get an intramuscular Neulasta shot to help my counts recover. This meant at least two needle pokes with each round of chemo, sometimes more.

I quickly got over my fear of needles. At first, I would start a conversation with my nurse or look at my phone or around the room to distract myself. Then, I practiced becoming comfortable by taking little peeks at the needle. After watching a few times, I decided I wanted to give myself my shot. I thought about it for a week before finally asking.

On the day I asked, I had been assigned to one of my favorite nurses, Rachael. Rachael supported me but wanted to get permission from my team first. In came Katherine, my sassy, fun-loving nurse practitioner. Katherine granted me permission to give myself my shot, but she wanted to make sure I understood that the medicine in this shot was extremely expensive and that insurance may not cover a backup, so I needed to be serious, and I could not waste the medicine.

A few quick minutes after promising that I would be careful and serious, Rachael was gloving up and passing me the shot. She showed me how to hold my skin before giving me the, "Ok, you ready, sweet girl?"

I nodded and she passed me the shot. I felt a little nervous, but I was determined to prove I could do this—prove it to myself, prove it to everybody. This was my chance to take control. *If I have to get these shots, I'll do it myself.*

I took a deep breath and plunged the needle into my thigh. Once the needle was in, I began to slowly push the syringe. In this moment, I learned how much more I preferred to give myself my shots than to have others administer them because I can more easily control the rate. The Neulasta medicine burns, and while some prefer the shot fast, I like it really slow—so slow that the burning is almost unnoticeable.

This led to me learning to access my port myself. Whenever I developed fevers, I had to immediately go to my hometown emergency room and have my port accessed to draw for cultures and start antibiotics. The problem was, most of my local ER nurses did not have much, if any, experience accessing ports. This motivated both of my parents, and later me, to learn the proper techniques.

Because Mother and I are night owls, it became common for my nurses to gather in my room late at night. One night, after my night nurse Jennifer's other assigned patients had gone to sleep, my mom asked if Jennifer would show her how to access my port. Jennifer retrieved a doll that nurses use to learn how to access ports and taught my mom, step by step, how to set up the sterile field and how to proceed with the tedious prep work, skipping only the actual needle poke step since the hardest part is creating and maintaining a sterile field. I stood over the two, videoing on my phone so we would have detailed instructions in case we were to forget the steps. We spent a great amount of time discussing potential scenarios for accessing the port and the best way to handle each.

The following week, Daddy took me to the clinic for labs and a dose of outpatient chemo. This was the next time that I was due to have my port accessed, and Daddy took the opportunity to learn. He was successful and eager to brag to Mother about being the first one to access my port. It was rare that Mother did not come to clinic with me, so while she was happily relieved that he had learned, she joked about how she wanted to be first. It was not long before she had her chance, and she too was successful.

After they both learned, although it was uncommon for most patients to learn how to access their own port, I decided I wanted to as well. My motivation was not as much out of necessity since both of my parents were trained, but rather out of the challenge. I always love a good challenge. I think that is part of the reason why it has been so easy to always make the decision to continue fighting. I love beating the odds and doing things others are not doing. So, accessing my own port with a 1.5 inch needle seemed like a great idea.

The placement location of the port in my chest made it nearly impossible to see. I was working with an odd angle. In truth though, the hardest part was putting on the sterile gloves. I was instructed to only touch the inside of the gloves, lest they become unsterile, making it difficult to adjust them. If I were to adjust the gloves in a way that felt most natural, that would involve my bare hands touching the sterile outside of the glove, thus breaking the sterility. The gloves were baggy on my hands, and I could hardly see over my mask when looking down at my chest. Not only do you have to hit the port underneath the skin, but you have to hit the very center. I did it all by feeling for the port and taking a deep breath. As I breathed out, I went against all natural reflexes and plunged the needle into my chest.

We tested if it was a success by drawing for blood return. When we saw red in the tubing, we all cheered, and the nurse helped me place a dressing over the port.

Mid-treatment for Ewing's, my first port flipped, making it useless. The top side, where the needle was supposed to enter, had flipped to face my insides and the outside was facing my skin. We first learned that it had flipped when I was admitted for another round of chemo and none of my nurses could access it. Most surgeries would take weeks or longer to schedule, but Dr. Stine called the surgery unit and I was scheduled the following morning to remove and replace the port so that I could continue chemo. This reinforced the emphasis ACH placed on the needs of oncology patients and the persistence of Dr. Stine, which played an important role in my treatment.

I was especially excited to learn that my favorite surgeon, Dr. Maxson, would be replacing my port so that I could continue chemo. I have worked with several general surgeons for small procedures over the years, and Dr. Maxson is fantastic. He listens to me and takes my opinions as the patient into consideration. Not only does he not use a condescending tone like many other surgeons, but he makes jokes and speaks with a friendly voice. Dr. Maxson was actually a friend of my grandfather Sam first. Dr. Maxson is the chief of the hospital's trauma program and is a consultant on trauma for the Department of Health, and Sam is an emergency room doctor, so the two had spent time together at meetings and conferences over the years. At some point, Sam had given Dr. Maxson a cartoonish, floppy hat with bright drawings.

On the morning of the port replacement, I was wheeled down to the OR. With my terrible eyesight, everything was blurry, as I did not have my contacts in or glasses on in preparation for surgery. I was lying on the OR table and the anesthesiologist had just placed a mask over my face. He was about to begin the sedation when the doors opened and Dr. Maxson entered. I could barely make out his face from the doorway but recognized his voice as he asked the anesthesiologist to wait. As he approached the OR table, I realized he was wearing the silly hat that my grandfather had gifted him. He had remembered to bring it on the day of my surgery and wanted a quick selfie. We both grinned toward his phone. My parents later told me they got a good laugh about the OR selfie while in the waiting room, and Daddy was able to pass it on to Sam, who enjoyed it as well.

I can only imagine what it must have been like for my parents and family to wait during all my surgeries. I always felt fortunate that I was the one to sleep through it instead of having to wait anxiously. I'm thankful for good doctors like Dr. Maxson who went above and beyond during my treatment to add levity. It would have been easy for him to just follow the routine and perform the surgery, but the few extra minutes he took helped set everyone at ease.

If you look closely, there are always opportunities for celebration, even in the hospital. One New Year's Eve, I planned a party for the other cancer kids admitted to 4K. I got the idea while bored and resting between infusions. I was visiting with my child life specialist, Emily, about how we all needed something upbeat to do that night. She was off work long before the stroke of midnight when the party would start, but she helped me set up everything before her shift ended. My parents and a couple of other patients' families brought in several dessert options, and Emily printed off games for us to play. We brought a TV into the unit's teen room so that we could all watch the ball drop, and Emily left the key with a nurse so that we could get in and celebrate after hours. The stage was set.

I set aside time to take a nap that evening while getting chemo so that I would be rested for the party. All the other kids and teens were excited, and my siblings were there to celebrate with us. Around 11:30 p.m., when the others were getting ready for the party to start, things got crazy in my room. My port infiltrated during my chemo infusion, meaning the chemo leaked out of the needle and onto my skin. We caught it early, but there were still some light burns. Unfortunately, after we reaccessed my port, we had to place a new dressing over the burns, which only irritated them further. It was a rush to reaccess before the clock struck midnight, but my nurses moved quickly and handled the situation. When it was time for me to head down the hall to the party, it was also time for another dose of IV Ativan to combat the nausea. I could barely stand up straight, but my nurses and family helped me down the hall. The party is a bit of a blur, but I remember seeing several smiling faces from my friends who were present, and I was excited about the ice cream cake. We all chanted down from ten as the clock approached midnight and the ball dropped.

For many, New Year's signifies change, but for me, every year that comes signifies celebration: celebration of another year survived, similar to the celebration of every new morning, but magnified—celebration of 365 new mornings and celebration of the hope for 365 more.

My nurses often joked that my hospital room entry was a revolving door. Many of my friends became frequent visitors. Maggie would always bring cupcakes, and I knew if Maddi or Anna visited, there would be lots of snuggles. My poor friend Luke sat through many *Toddlers and Tiaras* marathons and patiently listened to medicated-me vent about whatever was on my mind. Mrs. Renfrow made several surprise visits to pop in and check on me. She'd update me on what was going on in cheer, and I'd update her on my treatment. Anyone who stopped in during the 10 a.m. hour would be invited to watch Hoda, Kathie Lee, and Jenna on the TODAY show with me.

I have been blessed with a phenomenal support system of people who have not cared if I was sleeping, or medicated, or violently vomiting. They've loved me anyway. I would also make college friends who would brave visiting me in the hospital. I can only imagine how intimidating it must have been for them.

I am comfortable in the hospital and with the routines I've developed. It is a familiar setting that to me is like home, but I'm also aware that the constant beeping, nurses dashing in and out, and intense atmosphere can be daunting.

Naina, who I met through Instagram after beginning treatment, was already familiar with the hospital atmosphere. We met through our shared hobby of planning, as both of us enjoyed stickers, patterned tapes, and bright ink pens in our planners. I have always loved planners and anything that gives me a sense of organization. I can recall as far back as third grade when I went to Target for a toy and came out with a pink and orange color-block planner that had little rings, allowing me to move the pages around. There is a significant online community of people who decorate their planners as both a hobby and for productivity. A few months after receiving my cancer diagnosis, I was searching YouTube for possible sneak peeks of the anticipated Erin Condren planner release. I came across a few videos of people using stickers and tape (known as washi tape) in their planners, to make them both decorative and functional. From there, I fell down the rabbit hole. Not only did this lead me to Naina but to countless other amazing friends in the planner community.

Naina already had a huge following, but we clicked because we had something big in common. Naina was a resident just out of medical school who knew she wanted to treat cancer patients. She'd go on to become an oncologist. Our shared love of planners and all things pink combined with her passion to help others in similar circumstances as me was the foundation of our friendship. At first look, so many things were different about us. Naina grew up as a first-generation Indian in the Midwest and is ten years older than me. She lives in Chicago, a huge city differing greatly from my small Southern town. But we understand each other, almost as if our brains are wired in the same way. She's the big sister I never had.

I aim to be more like Naina in many ways, but mostly I want to be as kind and generous. Not long after we connected, she secretly began to reach out to others in the planner community to share my story. Telling them of my love of planning and organizing, she coordinated enormous donations of planner supplies from other "planner girls" all over the country.

When I arrived at the hospital for another round of chemo one day, there were several large boxes at the desk with my name on them. I was ecstatic to sort through the piles of stickers, washi tape, pen pouches, and planner bands. I spent hours sorting and even made a medicated live-stream video to thank Naina and everyone who gifted me the goodies. It felt heartening to be so connected into a community of virtual strangers with shared interests. This support meant I had people rooting for me from all over the country, people I had never met. I felt even more encouraged to keep fighting.

As time went on, so did the chemo. Eventually, March rolled around, and I had reached my last scheduled round. We wanted to celebrate big. The prep began during my next-to-last round. My amazing social worker, Carolyn, printed off pages and pages of Party City's online decoration options. I told her I would be sending my parents to get decor, and she was eager to help me pick out a heap of pink and gold accessories. We circled everything we wanted in bright highlighter and, when the last round came, sent the stack of papers with my parents. No space was left unadorned. Balloons filled the ceiling, and we decorated the windows leading out into the atrium with window paint. Pink and gold tablecloths and streamers were everywhere. Mother made me several posters with catchy quotes about the end of treatment and how much treatment I had completed.

Then came the dance parties. Everyone who entered my room was required to film a dance video with me, complete with props. I have so many selfies from the week-long party. I did not care that the chemo was flowing. I was celebrating! The festivities ended with a surprise party at my house when I arrived home. Maddi had worked again to surprise me with all of my close friends in my living room. I still cannot help but grin when thinking of that 17th round of chemo full of pink and gold feather boas, lots of cupcakes, and proud friends.

Once my counts recovered, I was granted permission to return to school. It was April of my senior year, and I had only signed up for one class. By Christmas, I had all the credits needed for graduation but decided to go ahead and take Pre-Cal/Trig so that I wouldn't have to take any math classes in college. I had been doing all of the work at home that semester. Each week, Bre would stop by my teacher's room to pick up my assignments and a copy of the class notes, exchanging them for the previous week's completed work.

There were only about three weeks of classes until graduation, and I went to math class for an hour and a half three days a week. While I worked from home throughout the school year, I like to joke that I skipped senior year because I attended fewer than a dozen classes.

Prom fell during the last bit of the school year. When the time came, Bre and Mother took me to Little Rock to spend the whole day shopping. We went from one dress shop to another trying on dresses in every color of the rainbow.

While it was probably obvious to some of the employees and other customers that I was a cancer kid because of my slick head, I am sure none of them knew I was taking prescription pain medicine around the clock that day. I was fresh out of treatment and the only side effect I was experiencing was a sore throat, likely from returning to school and being exposed to germs. My immune system was still weakened and was struggling to heal my throat. The pain was so bad that it hurt to breathe. It was manageable with pain medicine, but bad enough that when the medicine began to wear off I needed to immediately take another pill so that it did not become unbearable.

About midafternoon, we moved on to the next dress shop, Buffie's All The Rage, the same shop where I had found my homecoming gown. As I was trying on dresses in the fitting room, Buffie, the shop owner, pulled Mother aside and generously told Mother that she wanted to give me my prom dress. They decided to wait to tell me until I picked out my dress, that way the offer would not impact my decision on which dress to choose.

I had it narrowed down to an emerald-green gown and a rose-red dress. Both were nice contrasts to my dark eyes. I ended up choosing the red dress because it had more bling, and of course because it is my signature color.

Once I decided which dress I wanted, Buffie revealed that she would like to give it to me. She reminisced about the time from a few months back when I had been in her shop looking for my homecoming dress. She told me about the impact I had made on her as she embraced me in a hug. I still shake my head in amazement when I think about the goodwill Buffie showed me that day. So many people have gone out of their way over the years to show compassion in both big and small ways, and for that I will be eternally grateful.

Everything was coming together, and I was growing eager for prom. One school day during lunch, I was surprised to see Maddi and her boyfriend, Hunter, holding a poster board with pictures of Maddi and me at different ages. The poster read "Best friends at every stage, now can I make it on your planner page . . ." Next to those words was a prom checklist with all of the things a girl needs for prom checked off, except "date." Maddi and Hunter invited me to third-wheel prom with them. Of course, I said yes.

Finally, the day of prom arrived. Maddi picked me up, and Hunter joined us for group pictures. There was chatter of concerns with what the music selection might be that night, but I recall it being much better than expected. Afterward, Bre joined us for a late dinner at Texas Roadhouse, where we devoured cheese fries, in homage to the night we enjoyed cheese fries after first finding the mass.

As with most kids during their senior year, the time between prom and graduation blinked away. Nearly 15 months after I was diagnosed, I proudly walked with my class and received my high school diploma. Before my diagnosis, I never dreamed that I might not make it to graduation or that I would potentially graduate late. Cancer changed that. Achieving high school graduation was one of the first signs that I was making it. I was beating the odds.

To top off the excitement of the day, I was happily surprised to see three unexpected, yet familiar, faces in the audience. As I walked onto the floor to begin the ceremony, my face lit up as I saw my nurses, Rachael, Amber, and Jennifer, smiling from ear to ear and waving at me. Jennifer had mentioned to me over a year before that she was planning to attend my graduation. I had long forgotten her promise because it seemed like a big expectation for her to travel two hours to watch me graduate. Yet there she was, following through, with Rachael and Amber cheering me on by her side.

Afterward, my family and I went to dinner at a favorite

creole restaurant. As expected, it was a great dinner, but part of the excitement was the anticipation of an upcoming graduation gift—a trip to New Orleans with PaPaw the following week. It was the perfect end to a rocky senior year.

Gradually, I was regaining my strength.

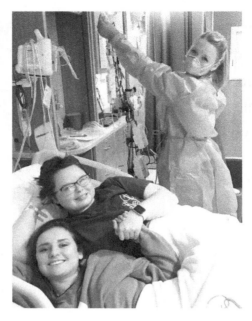

Nurse Amber starts chemo while Kaden and Maddi rest:
first round of chemo for leukemia

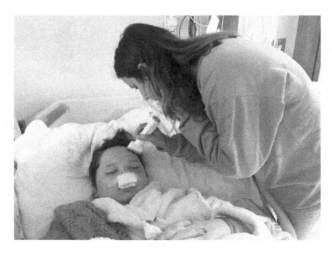

Maddi shaves Kaden's head . . . again

Kaden resting in ACH Pediatric Intensive Care Unit, trying to survive fungal infection

2,524 Beads of Courage, representing: 1 fungal infection; 2 allogeneic transplants; 2 rapid response calls (MET); 3 central lines; 3 ports; 4 lumbar punctures with chemo; 4 donor lymphocyte infusions; 9 line/port surgeries; 15 OR visits; 18 bone marrow biopsies; 33 sedations; 36 inpatient eye treatments; 37 days of IV nutrition; 40 radiation treatments; 46 nasal scopes; 49 ER visits; 81 dressing changes; 126 scans; 184 chemo infusions; 187 blood transfusions; 237 clinic visits; 249 nights in the hospital; 282 needle pokes; and 876 IV antibiotic infusions.

2015 True Scrapper Award. It reads:
"Scrapper: A fighter or aggressive competitor,
especially one always ready or eager for a fight."

Showing off Scrapper Jeans during chemo

Peebles Family Conquers Stonehenge
(Make-A-Wish Trip)

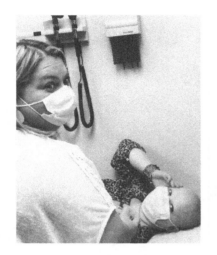
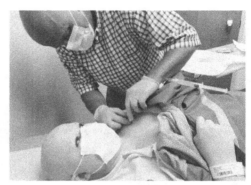

Michelle and Damon Peebles access Kaden's port for the first time

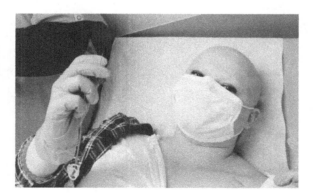

Kaden accesses her own port for the first time

The Wedding Party

The Bride and Groom

Kaden and Keagan reunited after
Transplant 1

Celebrating with PaPaw

College Graduation: Bre, Kaden, Andrew

Part 2

Summer filled my days with humidity and Netflix. After spending the previous year traveling only to the hospital, I became
eager to travel elsewhere.

The week I graduated, my parents and I went to Dallas to
attend a scholarship dinner for a foundation named "1 Million
4 Anna," started by David and Carol Basso in memory of their
daughter Anna, who had been diagnosed with Ewing's Sarcoma. Wanting to make a difference in their grief, they founded 1
Million 4 Anna to fund Ewing's Sarcoma research, stock closets
with gifts for teens fighting cancer at countless hospitals, and
provide college scholarships for Ewing's Sarcoma fighters and
survivors.

Being in a room full of other Ewing's Sarcoma survivors
and their families that night was an indescribable feeling. There
were teens and young adults slick bald, others with long, flowy
hair, and many in between, representing the different stages of

life post-treatment. While I would never wish this diagnosis on my worst enemy, it was peaceful to be able to relate to so many people at one time, in one place.

I met two remarkable young women there, Lauren and Kyla. Both were fighting Ewing's Sarcoma, and not for the first or even second time. Lauren had long dark hair and was in school at Texas A&M. Mother and I had been following Lauren's story through the blog she and her mom shared. Mother came across it late one night while in the hospital with me, and it was the blog that first connected us to the 1 Million 4 Anna Foundation. Lauren was one of the first people I saw fighting cancer for an extended period, giving me the inspiration to fight too. I read in her blogs that she was always eager and willing to try any new treatment, which made me eager to try new treatments, even if they seemed scary.

Kyla was the guest speaker that night and was one of the kindest souls I have ever met. We instantly bonded and learned we had the same monogram, KPA. Kyla wore a head wrap around her bald head, which I later learned was not to conceal her lack of hair, but to cover protruding tumors. She shared her story and concluded with naming all of the physical locations that the cancer had infiltrated. It seemed as if there was not one spot she didn't mention: her skull, her lungs, most of her bones, her liver, her lymph nodes . . . The cancer was everywhere. I thought that my one localized tumor was bad. I thought wrong.

After the event, Kyla and I stayed in touch, texting often, and she even wanted to visit me once doctors told her there was nothing more they could do for her. I also stayed in touch with Lauren and watched for updates on her blog and her mother's Facebook page.

Both girls died within the year to Ewing's Sarcoma. *Why them and not me?* I wondered.

Since that dinner, the Basso family has remained a huge part of my life. They have continued to provide me with educational scholarships, follow my updates, and visit me in the hospital. I am so grateful for my connection with David and Carol, as well as their oldest daughter, Patrice. Although I never had the pleasure of meeting Anna, I can only imagine how proud she would be of her family. They worked to build a foundation and continue her legacy, all while inspiring me and others to turn grief into change.

The week following graduation, PaPaw took me to New Orleans for my first planner conference. Since my post-diagnosis obsession with planners began, I had joined several Facebook groups and followed many "planner grams"—Instagram accounts dedicated to planning—which led to me create my own account and attend national planner conferences.

New Orleans was the first location where the Facebook group known as Planners Gone Wild hosted their annual conference. In just five short years, the conference tripled in size. Thanks to Naina, the administration team, and PaPaw, I have been there since the start.

Naina was a speaker that year, sharing how she incorporates healthy eating and exercise into her planning routine. She was able to snag me a ticket as her guest, and PaPaw took care of the rest. I left NOLA with a sneak peek of that year's upcoming Erin Condren planner release, a selfie with the founder Erin Condren herself, tons of planners and planner accessories, new lifelong friendships, and a grateful heart for a weekend with my PaPaw.

That weekend, PaPaw and I had a few free hours between conference activities and decided to check out the World War II Museum. We both agreed we could have easily spent a whole day there, exploring all of the artifacts.

A couple of weeks after visiting the World War II Museum in New Orleans, my family and I were able to visit the Churchill Museum in London and view the British perspective of the same war. The Churchill Museum had countless interactive features, and I even walked through a replica of the bunker Churchill stayed in during the war. Having a family composed of boys and girls with varying ages, it can sometimes be challenging to find an activity that everyone is equally interested in, but the Churchill Museum definitely intrigued all five of us.

This opportunity was made possible thanks to Make-A-Wish. As a result of my Ewing's Sarcoma diagnosis, I was granted a wish—anything I wanted. I thought about several things, like meeting Beyoncé or visiting the set of *The Vampire Diaries*, but ultimately, I knew I wanted to do something that would last more than one day and that would include my entire family.

So often when one is diagnosed with cancer, the family is forgotten. While many were asking how I was doing, my siblings were rarely asked how they were making it. The focus naturally shifted to me, but in reality, their lives were shuffled and flipped upside down as well. My parents were often away at the hospital, and PaPaw had to transition from grandparent to parent for my siblings. Consistency and routine halted. They spent every weekend and school break in the hospital with me. While I know their sacrifices were gladly given, I felt they should be rewarded. What better way than to share my wish?

So, I wished for a European family vacation. Make-A-Wish came through and gifted us a trip to London, Paris, and Rome during the summer post-graduation and treatment. We joked that we were like the Griswolds from *National Lampoon's European Vacation*, and in all actuality, we probably were. We stood out like sore thumbs with our Arkansan accents and customs, but the experiences were gratifying.

My favorite city was Rome. The food was to die for, and the ornate details in the architecture captivated me, as did the shopping. As I walked through the streets, I often heard music, and the sun felt extra warm. I noticed everyone walked everywhere and my "when in Rome" walking burned off all of the Italian carbs I devoured.

While it was probably pretty obvious that we were touring, there was one moment in Rome when Daddy passed for a local. On the hotel elevator with another American and an Italian, the American woman was having difficulties working the elevator. When she stepped off, the Italian woman looked at Daddy and made a comment alluding to "stupid Americans." He just grinned and verbally agreed, revealing his American dialect. The woman instantly knew that she had been bad-mouthing Americans to an American, and she looked mortified. To make the day even more ironic, the woman was on our day-long tour of the Colosseum. Daddy could not help but grin every time she made eye contact with him.

From London, we had plans to take a bus ride to Stonehenge. The scheduled departure time came and ticked away. Finally, after nearly two hours of waiting, the bus arrived. Not far into the trip, the driver came over the speaker to inform us that he had exceeded the limit of consecutive hours he could legally drive.

After an hour pulled over and a long drive, we were finally approaching Stonehenge. We peered out the windows at the grassy green fields with sheep grazing away. We could faintly see the giant stones in the distance when the bus driver's voice echoed over the bus speakers again, informing us that he was turning around. He had just gotten off the phone with the people at Stonehenge, and it was too close to closing time for us to visit. Suddenly, he made a nail-biting U-turn on the busy highway. On the trip back to London, passengers began chatting. Most of us were tourists, saddened not only because we wouldn't be visiting one of the Wonders of the World, but also because we had lost nearly a whole day of valuable travel time. One woman shared how she had the exact same experience the previous day in another attempt to see Stonehenge and had now lost two days.

Just as the news was setting in, the bus driver picked up his microphone and spoke again. He had managed to talk Stonehenge into letting us come for a few minutes. With his second U-turn, the bus erupted with clapping and sighs of relief. As we pulled in, he announced that we had thirty minutes until we needed to be back at the bus, and he was leaving right on the dot.

There were carts driving passengers from the bus to the stones about half a mile away, but they quickly filled up and we didn't have time for everyone to wait on a ride. My family and I instantly began making our way toward the exhibit on foot. My siblings and Mother took off running, while Daddy stayed behind with me. I moved as quickly as possible. My body was still weak from the treatment, but I had spent the last month walking laps around the school's track, training my body to be strong again. Mother had gone with me to the track, and often she would link arms with me and pull me along. She had pushed me to push myself, and I have no doubt that if it weren't for her, my feet would not have carried me the countless miles we would walk throughout Europe.

Despite multiple obstacles, my family and I made it to the towering stones. We captured selfies and pondered the mystery. Who put them there and why? It was fun to discuss hypotheses.

After viewing them, we were able to catch a ride back on

one of the carts and even had enough time to pick out souvenirs before heading back to London.

Today, we cannot help but laugh about the events that unfolded the day we visited Stonehenge. These were the kind of memories I had in mind when I wished to visit Europe with my family.

Another happened in Paris, when a famous, unexpected guest arrived. A petite American lady on tour of the Louvre with us had mentioned a bakery called Angelina's and how delicious its cocoa and macarons are. My family decided to take her advice and visit the bakery for dessert and hot chocolate that evening.

As we stepped through the ceiling-to-floor drapes framing the front door, we discovered Angelina's was standing-room-only small with treat-lined glass cases and a handful of busy baristas. From inside, everything we saw through the glass doors appeared normal, but while we ordered macarons and cocoa, chaos ensued outside. As we exited, we noticed a hotel immediately to the right of the bakery doors and police had the sidewalk blocked off in that direction. The street was also blocked off, and countless black SUVs with tinted windows began lining it. Men with black suits and dark sunglasses were parking and running down the street toward the hotel. A red carpet was rolled out in front of the hotel, and people crowded around as close as the police allowed. The crowd began questioning what was going on, and a female officer informed us that the president of Korea was visiting. We all looked around with big eyes and wondered aloud, "Which Korea?" It was soon mentioned that the South Korean president was the guest visitor. After a few minutes of chaos, we saw the man of the hour come forward from a vehicle and quickly enter the hotel. While the entrance itself was nothing grand, the preparation for the president to enter the hotel was unlike anything we'd ever seen.

The trip was a memory we will hold forever. Whenever I reflect on it, I think of the many other kids and teens with life-threatening illnesses who are granted once-in-a-lifetime experiences from Make-A-Wish. I knew the trip would be something I would value, but I had no way to predict how much our family would cherish it during times shadowed by the unknown.

When mid-August rolled around, I was eager to move out for the first time. I enrolled in classes at Texas A&M University–Texarkana, only an hour from home, and began dorm-room shopping.

The dorms were fairly new and spacious. Due to a weakened immune system from treatment, I had my own room. I pushed the twin beds together to make a king-size bed and luxuriated in having my own double vanity bathroom, two closets, and full-size couch.

Not only was my room great, but so was my life. I signed up for a gym membership and went to Target and ULTA often. I could go to Starbucks or Chick-fil-A when I pleased and was surrounded by new friends. I even got a part-time job teaching preschool gymnastics at the gym where I had taken tumbling classes and done competitive cheer. Because I was only an hour from home, I could still see family regularly, no matter the day.

I was also blessed with extended family members in Texarkana. My great-aunt and great-uncle, Tish and Larry (who had read my MRI during my Ewing's diagnosis), lived minutes from my dorm. I have always been close to them, and my dad has always had a special relationship with them too. I knew I could pop over at any time and Aunt Tish would fix me a dinner plate, take me along on whatever errands she was running, or just sit on the couch and visit.

While I remained optimistic that I was moving on from cancer, fears loomed in the back of my mind as well. My main concern was a relapse of bone cancer.

When I began having headaches, I attributed it to my more active schedule and decreased sleep. It made sense; I was adjusting to college. Then, when my blood counts dropped slightly, I attributed it to a weakened immune system and living in a dorm and being exposed to more germs. Plus, I had always heard through the "pediatric cancer grapevine" that a sign of leukemia—a secondary cancer that I knew could potentially be caused by the chemotherapy and radiation I had undergone—is elevated blood counts. One afternoon, I told Mother, "At least I don't have leukemia, because my counts are low."

Soon, the headaches got so bad that I struggled to function. I spent days missing class and planned events. I could barely hold my head up, but I told myself that headaches and fatigue were normal. My scans remained good, so I had no reason to worry. Just five days after clear scans, my symptoms pressed on.

One day in early October, PaPaw met me outside my dorm and took me to get a new phone because mine had broken. Afterward, he took me out for one of my favorite lunches at Bryce's Cafeteria. We ate a home-cooked meal and had a great visit.

Despite the wonderful day and my will to feel happy, I was grumpy. While irritability is not a textbook symptom for extremely low blood counts, it should have been my sign. Whenever my counts would drop because of chemo, I would easily grow irritable. I hated it, but it's difficult to be patient and happy when you are low on blood and not getting good oxygen flow.

PaPaw was patient as always and didn't even acknowledge my grumpiness. After he left, I decided to rest before my late-afternoon class. While lying down on the couch and resting, my breathing was labored. My chest pounded as if I had just run a marathon, only I hadn't done any activity. *I should call Mother*, I thought, unsure and anxious about my physical symptoms.

"Hello?" said her voice on the other end.

"Hey, I kinda feel like I have low counts."

"What makes you think that?" she asked.

"My head is pounding, and it feels a little hard to breathe. I've just been lying on the couch and my lungs are labored. I can feel my blood pumping. I'm just really tired."

"Okay . . . " I could tell in her voice that she was processing this information while also trying to reassure me.

171

"I haven't done anything to make me feel this way. And I've been kinda grumpy today for no reason. PaPaw has been here, we had a nice visit, and I even got a new phone." I knew she would understand the significance of me being grumpy.

"Just hang tight and wait for us to get there."

When we got off the phone, I walked to class and sat through a biology lecture. After class, I met Mother. Agreeing I wasn't in a good state, we made the decision to have lab work done. I informed my boss that I wouldn't be at work for the next two days, then drove back to my dorm. Even if my labs were alright, I would go home for a few days to rest. I laid my large suitcase open on my dorm room floor and scurried around, throwing clothes into it.

Then, Mother and Bre picked me up and drove me home to Nashville, where I went to the local hospital. The set of labs Sam ordered confirmed that something was wrong. My hemoglobin was 6. Normal was 12 to 14. I had only half of the amount of blood that I should.

Mother drove us home, where Daddy greeted me with a bear hug. We called the oncologist-on-call line and reached Dr. Do, a kind physician who had treated me before. Dr. Do's deep voice echoed through the phone as he asked me a few questions regarding my symptoms. He told me that I could decide if I wanted to admit to the hospital through the ER for a blood transfusion that night or wait and come to clinic the following morning. We decided to go ahead and admit.

We arrived at the ER in Little Rock after midnight and

eventually settled in my room on 4K. That was one of the most bittersweet moments I have ever experienced. I was happy to see my nurses again, but I thought I was done with staying in the hospital. I was supposed to be better.

The following morning, the two oncologists on call for the week, Dr. Crary and Dr. Do, entered my room for rounds. After we greeted each other for the first time in a while, the tone of the room shifted.

"We aren't quite sure why you are needing extra blood transfusions, but the good thing is you are responding well," reassured Dr. Crary in her soft voice.

I nodded.

"There are a few things that could be going on," continued Dr. Do. "Your counts could be low due to a possible infection. If that's the case, your body is fighting it and using all your blood cells. It could also be a reaction to the Bactrim. How long have you been taking it?"

Bactrim, my weekly preventative antibiotic. "About a year now," I answered.

"So that could be the cause. Or the third thing . . ." Dr. Do trailed off.

I already knew. We all knew. That's why I was in this specific hospital on this specific floor with these specific doctors.

Dr. Crary picked up where Dr. Do left off, ". . . It could be a secondary cancer. Leukemia. The chances are slim though. It may be a good idea to do a bone marrow biopsy to rule this out." Everyone in the room nodded as my parents and I agreed.

"Would you rather go ahead and do it while you are here or wait?"

I inhaled, "Let's just go ahead and get it out of the way so we will know."

"Okay, we'll get it scheduled in the morning." Dr. Crary gave me a soft smile and murmured okays and goodbyes.

It felt good to see my people, but now I had to wait until the next day. I questioned why somebody in my position would opt to wait longer when the uncertainty of waiting a day to see what was going on seemed like torture enough.

Waking up in my dark hospital room after the biopsy, I struggled to keep my eyes open through a blur of sedation and pain medications. My parents sat on the couch near my hospital bed. After a while, Dr. Crary, Dr. Do, and my child life specialist, Emily, entered the room. Dr. Do held his head low, and Dr. Crary did not have her usual grin and sparkly eyes. While I am always delighted to see Emily, I knew her presence wasn't a good sign. Child life does many things, one of which is to help inform patients and their families of bad news.

On October 7, exactly one year to the day after I learned of my Ewing's remission, I received my second cancer diagnosis: Secondary Acute Myeloid Leukemia. It was crazy to think that just a few days before I was doing my daily activities like going to the gym, getting a new phone, and attending class. Suddenly, I was snapped out of the world of the healthy and plunged back into the world of cancer. I thought I had escaped but was back to ground zero in the blink of an eye.

Having made many friends who were in treatment for leukemia, I was somewhat familiar with it. I knew that leukemia
is often divided into two categories and subcategories from
there. One category includes high-dose chemotherapy over a
shorter period of time, usually less than six months, depending
on setbacks. The other is similar but is often followed by a few
years of maintenance therapy. Maintenance usually consists of
monthly lumbar punctures with chemo injected in the spine,
as well as oral chemo pills and steroids. While maintenance
means several years of treatment and many tough days, some
of my friends in maintenance had been able to return to school
and grow their hair out during this period.

One of my first questions was to clarify this information
and find out if I would need maintenance treatment.

"You know too much for someone getting a new diagnosis," Dr. Crary shook her head. "Chemo alone won't get you to

remission. Because this is a secondary cancer caused by your treatment, you'll need a stem cell transplant."

Several kids I knew had needed to go out of state for transplants, so I knew this was something that Arkansas would not be able to give me.

Between questions, I was fading in and out. My parents and doctors agreed to step into a conference room to further discuss what this meant, and Emily stayed to comfort me while I rested.

Before they left, my eyes searched for Mother through the darkness, and I called out to her. When she came near, I managed to whisper, "God is not done with me."

She cried out, reassuring me, "Oh, Kaden! No, He isn't!"

"Not in a bad way. He still has plans for me. He's using this. He has something better in mind."

Mother laughed out loud, reassured. I think she interpreted "done with me" as a reference to death, which was true in a sense, but I meant it differently. We were all still processing what was unfolding, but I knew at that moment that this diagnosis would be something bigger than just me. I had faith that this bad would bring opportunity to encourage others. Even in these moments I knew God was with me, and I had faith that He was using this for good that I could not yet comprehend. This faith in Him during the unknown was my rock many days.

After Mother and Daddy left for one of the few conversations they'd have with my doctors out of my presence, I looked up from my hospital bed and saw Emily's face through the dark.

She looked as if she was aiming to remain calm, but there was sadness in her eyes. She sat with me for what felt like forever and answered my slurred questions. I learned that my siblings would be tested to see how close a match our DNA is and that I would need to go out of state. Of the kids I knew who had gone off for transplant, many had gone to Dallas.

At one point, I woke up and Dr. Audrey Green-Murphy was standing to the right of my hospital bed with Mother at her side. I was relieved to see her. At the time, she was a third-year fellow, and she would later go on to specialize in the study and treatment of pediatric brain cancer. Not only is she easily one of the smartest people I have ever met, but she is also incredibly compassionate.

My primary oncologist, Dr. Stine, is amazing and brilliant, but I had always thought that if something happened and he could no longer be my doctor, I would want Dr. Green-Murphy to be my primary oncologist. I also knew that while Dr. Stine is a pediatric oncologist, he specializes in sarcomas, and I now had a different diagnosis. With this in mind, I looked at Dr. Green-Murphy through the fuzzy lens of post-sedation medication and asked, "Are you my doctor now?"

She chuckled. "No, Dr. Stine is still your primary oncologist."

Mother gave me a soft smile and informed me, "She's just here to check on you."

She was standing there not because she was my primary doctor or the doctor on call but because she cared. She took time out of her busy day to comfort my parents and me.

"Do you know if I'll need to have surgery to get another port placed?"

"No, but you'll need a Broviac catheter."

"The tubes that some of my friends with leukemia had?"

"Yes, it allows you to receive more infusions simultaneously. Lots of leukemia patients require more medications and infusions, so this makes it easier."

One of my nurses would later explain that this was more commonly known as a central line. It would be similar to the port, in the sense that I would draw labs and receive medications and transfusions through it, but differ in that the tube would hang from my chest until it was surgically removed. The tubing would technically consist of two tubes, so that I could simultaneously receive infusions and transfusions without an unwanted interaction.

Dr. Green-Murphy also cleared up some confusion I had and explained that stem cell transplants are used in oncology patients when they relapse or when a secondary cancer develops—the latter being my case.

Dr. Stine was out of town that weekend, but Dr. Green-Murphy had contacted him to inform him of the unwanted results. His response, passed via Dr. Green-Murphy: "Damn." Dr. Stine had always seemed so formal and had excellent bedside manner, but in that moment he seemed real and relatable because we were each silently responding with our own swear words. Despite the fact that his response was not said directly to me, that barrier between patient and doctor was broken, and I appreciated it.

My nurse practitioner, Katherine, spent a great amount of time in my hospital room that afternoon as well. She was there for emotional support, as well as to help answer the series of questions forming.

As the afternoon passed, my parents and I decided that Mother should go home for the evening to be there when Bre cheered at the football game and to break the news to both of my siblings.

My doctors wanted to keep me overnight for an MRI of my brain. Because I had been having migraines, they wanted to make sure the leukemia had not crossed the brain-body barrier.

Daddy stayed with me, and we ate chicken strips while waiting on the MRI results. Dr. Mack stopped by my room after the scan. At the time, she was one of my fellows, and she went on to become one of my attending doctors. She let me know that the MRI looked good and took the time to see how I was doing emotionally. After a day of bad news, this negative scan felt extremely relieving.

Dr. Mack is one of the kindest souls. She has a soft voice and a way of soothing an aching heart, sitting at the end of my bed whenever she enters my hospital room and always listening to what I say with open ears. I knew that she was also a Christian, so I asked her to pray with me. She guided me in prayer and encouraged me to pray first, giving my worries to God. Then, she followed with a plea for healing, making me feel safe.

I was also blessed to be assigned to one of my favorite nurses that night, Faith. Once Faith's other patients were settled, she came to my bedside. She sat with me as my closest friends called in anticipation of the results. Maddi and Maggie each called, and while I did not tell them the news out of respect for my siblings who did not know yet, I did ask them to pray. I knew they would know by my response. Once I confirmed that my siblings knew and I could tell them, Faith held my hand as I proceeded to share.

The following day, I was discharged with strict instructions to not spend time in public to avoid germs. I was also told to gather my items from my dorm and spend time with family. I had approximately 36 hours to go home, pack, and prepare for battle.

Daddy and I left the hospital and headed to my dorm in Texarkana. My family would move all of my belongings out later, but I needed to gather clothes and other items for a long hospital stay. I could tell that Daddy felt just as heartbroken as I did. He is a quiet man, but he seemed even more quiet. His energy was low, and he sighed deeply.

PaPaw met us at my dorm, and when I stepped out of Daddy's truck, I felt my face grow puffy and my eyes fill with tears. I had worked so hard to get to this point, and now I was having to leave college. PaPaw wrapped his arms around me. Whenever PaPaw gives big bear hugs, they really feel bear-like, probably in large part because he is six-foot-nine. He reassured me it would be okay, but I know him well enough to know he is only ever positive. That was his line, "Positive, positive, positive!"

A high school friend who lived in the same dorms met me outside my dorm room door. She gave me a big hug and helped me sort through what I needed to take with me and what could be retrieved later. We loaded up, and I gave Daddy my dorm room key. He returned later with PaPaw and Andrew, and the boys who lived across the hall from me helped them move out the rest of my belongings. That would be the last time I would ever see my dorm room.

The rest of the weekend flashed by as I spent time with family and packed for what would come to be the toughest hospital stay of my life.

37

My parents and I returned to the hospital to meet with Dr. Stine for the first time since my leukemia diagnosis a few days before. The three of us were in the waiting room when Dr. Stine walked out and quickly greeted us. Usually, a nurse escorts the patients to a clinic room and gets them settled before they see the doctor. There have been very few times when I've seen Dr. Stine enter the waiting area, and this was one. He told us he was making some phone calls for me and proposed that we go to lunch and return that afternoon, allowing time for him to do some more research.

When we returned mid-afternoon, Dr. Stine presented three options for transplant locations. He had researched each and checked to see which one my insurance would approve. The first option was University of Arkansas for Medical Sciences (UAMS), ACH's sister hospital for adults in Little Rock. Dr. Stine said that the program was fairly new, he did not feel comfortable sending me there considering my case, and the doctor there also recommended we search for other options. The second option was St. Jude in Memphis, four hours from home. The third was Dr. Haydar Frangoul in Nashville, Tennessee, eight hours from home.

My parents asked Dr. Stine where he would send his child if they were in my situation, and Dr. Stine recommended Dr. Frangoul. The two had met while studying at Duke. Dr. Frangoul had gone on to study in Seattle, the mecca of transplant. He also helped build the transplant program at Vanderbilt and had moved to a second children's hospital in Nashville to build another transplant program there. His resume was outstanding, and I would soon learn he loves a good challenge, something I would be able to provide him.

It was also decided that right away, I'd do a round of mitoxantrone. This chemo stood out because it was blue-tinged, as opposed to the traditional clear consistency. I recall debating with my friend Omari whether the "red devil" chemo or the blue chemo was worse, as I had taken the red and he had taken the blue. This led to joking that since I was going to have both, I would determine which was nastier once and for all. (The conclusion? They are both pretty gnarly. You feel like you've been hit by a freight truck. Every muscle is sore, and you have no energy. You feel icky from the inside out, and the fatigue is extreme whether you take the red chemo *or* the blue chemo.)

With my port removed, I needed a way to infuse the blue chemo. I admitted to 4K and was scheduled with the OR to have my central line placed.

Back in my hospital room on 4K the following day, I was delighted to see my nurse Amber's face. Amber had given me my very first chemo infusion, and she would also give me my first chemo infusion against leukemia. While we were waiting for the chemo to arrive on the floor, a much sweeter arrival surprised me. Maddi had driven three hours from Fayetteville to Little Rock when she finished class that morning to spend the day with me.

Maddi climbed in bed with me as Amber entered the room to administer my chemo. Amber wore a plastic gown and special mask and was double gloved. Maddi and I spent the infusion cutting up, until the sickness kicked in. I had received my special anti-nausea cocktail and was making it okay. Despite the many blue bag breaks, the gossip was flowing.

Over the following days, my siblings and I had our cheeks swabbed to see how well our DNA matched. It took time to get the results back, but neither Bre nor Andrew were as close a match as we would have liked. Bre was a 5/10 match and Andrew was a 7/10 match. A 10/10 was ideal, a 9 would work, and an 8 would be our last option. Andrew's 7/10 just wasn't high enough. My parents offered to be tested, but since they each make up one half of my genetics, it would not be enough. There was mention of taking Daddy's cells and altering them in some way, if we were to have problems finding a match on the world-wide registry. Luckily, I had several 10/10 matches there.

Within two weeks, for the first time in treatment, I began to lose my appetite. Daddy, PaPaw, and Andrew had finished moving my belongings out of my dorm. Daddy and Mother swapped shifts, with Mother going home to unpack my belongings and Daddy coming to stay with me at the hospital. I vividly remember sitting in bed, entirely dependent on the back of the bed to support me. I was too weak to hold my head up. Daddy was begging me to eat. He had gone to the store and gotten me several types of soups, hoping something would sit well. I just did not have the willpower to open my mouth and eat.

Mother had picked up some fall wall scents from Bath & Body Works. One was Halloween scented, and while I don't know the name of it, the thick scent is engraved on my brain. It nauseates me to the point of gagging when thinking about it, because my brain associates that scent with vomiting.

During those days, I mostly only woke up to go to the bathroom. It seems like I spent a lot of time in the restroom, likely because I slept the rest of the time, so that is all that my memory allows. I was so weak that my nurses had to physically carry me to the shower and bathe me. I have never felt so vulnerable in my life. The nurses treated me with dignity. They never made me feel bad for not being able to take care of myself but rather helped me feel better despite the situation.

While only a couple of weeks had passed, this was the longest period I had spent in the hospital. No sunlight and little human interaction will do the brain bad. This combined with continuous narcotics caused me to have nightmares related enough to what I was going through physically that it was almost impossible to differentiate dreams from real life.

In my recurring dream, I was on a boat in the ocean, the boat rocking as I slept. A woman kept waking me, telling me to get to work. When I asked her how I got there, she forced me to clean the boat. After many variants of this dream, I always awoke in the hospital and asked how I got there. Was relapsing or the boat or both just a series of dreams? When I tried to grasp reality, there was nothing but rocking and rocking and rocking.

Even more difficult was trying to verbally express what I was going through mentally. I am not sure that I ever successfully explained to anyone during that time how confused I was.

At some point, we had started a morphine pain pump. I received a continuous flow of morphine and also had a button that I could press to administer more. There was a limit calculated by dosing and time, but my medical team was able to gauge my pain level based on how often the button was hit.

One night, I felt like I had been cut open. It was as if my chest was being repeatedly stabbed and could collapse any moment. I could hardly stay awake to press the button, but would wake up screaming in pain if the button was not pressed. For days, my family took shifts at my bedside, watching the clock and pressing the button so that my pain would be semi-managed.

When the weeks turned to weekends, my siblings, Pa-

Paw, and whichever parent was not at the hospital would all come to sit with me.

One weekend I still wasn't eating, so the doctors began infusing IV lipids through my central line to assure I'd still get nutrients. This also kept my appetite satisfied and made it difficult to start eating again. We were ordering takeout from one of my favorite restaurants, Homer's. Mother was asking everyone what they wanted to eat, so that she could call in the food.

"What about you, Kaden?" she asked, hopeful.

"Oh, I'm not really hungry," I said, looking down, knowing that my words would disappoint.

Mother pressed her lips together and moved on. Bre was lying next to me, and this was not acceptable to her. She rumpled her face and sternly asked me what I wanted to eat.

I whispered, "Bre, I'm not really eating right now."

She scrunched her eyebrows together even more. Her voice got kind of silly and soft. "I know you aren't . . . but you are going to eat tonight. "

Grudgingly, I agreed to order something. "Okay, but only a bite or two." I couldn't tell her no.

She smirked and whispered back, "What sounds good?"

I thought for a minute. I could hear my parents and Andrew discussing what they would eat, oblivious to the quiet conversation Bre and I were having.

Bre stared at me, waiting. I looked back at her and said, "Hmm, maybe rice..."

". . . with brown gravy?" She finished my sentence.

I nodded. She knew that I love rice with brown gravy.

"What about a vegetable plate? Maybe some macaroni?"

I sighed. "Sure."

"And green beans. You like green beans?"

I sighed out an, "Okayyy," then turned to Mother. She was picking up her phone to call in the food. "I'll have a vegetable plate."

She looked at me and stopped her movement. "What! You want to order something?"

"Yeah, Bre said I have to." Mother grinned back at me as I continued, "A vegetable plate with rice with brown gravy, macaroni, green beans . . . and maybe another thing?"

"What about greens?" Mother added with a hopeful tone.

"Yeah, that would be okay. I have to pick four. Just a few bites though. I *only* promised that I would try."

Mother nodded and picked up her phone to order before I could change my mind. As I rolled over, I noticed her giving Bre a nod.

While I hardly touched my food that night, I did have a couple of bites, and I give credit to Bre for kicking my appetite back on track.

My ears began bothering me. I've always had small ear canals, and it's typical for me to get ear infections. Whenever they bother me during treatment, I always mention it to my doctors. A couple of the doctors on the floor looked and agreed there might be a little fluid but no infection.

Then, my face began to feel stuffy, like I had a sinus infection. I searched on Pinterest for ways to relieve sinus pressure. While I saw some options, none seemed plausible, but I did gain some knowledge of how the sinuses work and connect.

I continued complaining about how uncomfortable my face felt, but my doctors concluded that it was likely just congestion. For a while, it was easy enough to convince myself.

Just to be safe, Dr. Sicente, the oncologist attending on call, proposed we do a CT of my face. The CT results came back fine. I was fine. Yet, the congestion pressure grew. One evening, I kept joking that I felt like my face was swollen, particularly the left side of my upper cheek and nose area. In my heart, I truly believed that I was only being dramatic.

When my nurse Kathleen came in to get routine vitals, she checked my temperature. I had a low-grade fever. For a while, my temperature hung out just below 101, just high enough that my entire body ached but just low enough that oncology protocol directed waiting to draw cultures and administer Tylenol. As I tossed and turned between Kathleen's fever checks, the pain in my face grew. Still, I tried to reassure myself that the CT showed nothing, and I was fine.

Kathleen continued to sneak into the darkness of my room, being careful not to wake Mother. In the wee hours of the morning, my fever hit 101. Kathleen followed protocol and drew cultures, then administered Tylenol.

As Kathleen was finishing, I woke Mother and informed her my fever had hit 101. I asked her to help me to the restroom. Only half awake herself, Mother rose from bed to help me through the darkness and into the low light of the bathroom nightlight.

As I was using the restroom, Mother stood in the doorway waiting to help me back to bed. Her eyes suddenly grew big and she flipped on all of the bathroom lights.

"Kaden! Look at me!"

She immediately turned around and headed toward the hallway. I wondered what was going on and figured she must have seen something worrisome, but I didn't have the strength to stand and look in the mirror. Within moments, Kathleen and most of the other nurses working that night shift surrounded me in the bathroom.

A barrage of questions began:

"Does it hurt?"

"What do your cheeks feel like?"

"Does your face feel heavy?"

"Can you breathe?"

They all oohed and ahhed with concern and intrigue.

Apparently, my face had swelled up like a basketball and was burning red. Everything was not fine. Kathleen phoned the doctor on call. Only a few hours remained until all of the doctors would be in, so Kathleen monitored me and Mother and I tried to rest.

Neither of us slept much, and closer to shift change, we were wide awake. I was steadily filling a bedside trash can with tissues, trying to blow my nose and relieve the pressure without success.

When the clock rolled over to dayshift, Tiffany was my nurse. Sharp and soft-spoken, Tiffany is everything a patient would want in a nurse in an emergent situation. She rarely left my side that day as we waited for an ENT to examine my face. They were dragging their feet, and the tension was building.

Tiffany was assessing the situation when she looked up at me. Her voice was calming, yet serious. "Are you scared?"

This is when I realized the severity of my situation. In my experience, nurses don't just throw the word "scared" around, and I knew Tiffany would only ask me if there was a reason.

"Maybe a little. Are you?"

She gulped. "I'm concerned that the swelling will increase and your airway may close."

I nodded.

"Kaden, I am going to do everything I can to take care of you. I need you to keep telling me what is going on though so I can do my very best."

I nodded again. I appreciated her honesty. The severity of the circumstances was becoming increasingly clear.

Tiffany was persistent in calling ENT as nurses circled in and out of my room. They each observed my face along with Mother and commented on the swelling with every passing second. Finally, an ENT surgery fellow entered my room. At first, he seemed agitated to have to leave the OR. He came rushing in, seemingly so he could quickly breeze through and return to what he was doing elsewhere. Very tall, he moved like a bull in a china cabinet. When he laid eyes on my face, there was an *aha* moment in his eyes that there was actually a legitimate reason to be called out of the OR.

Later that day, another CT scan was done, as well as a nasal scope. It was confirmed. I had a fungal infection that could potentially be fatal.

Days blurred into weeks.

I spent a lot of time with the ENT fellow, the physician in charge of doing my regular scopes. I never called him by his name, only Bama Boy, as he was from Alabama. Bama Boy was cute with dark hair and dark eyes. He likely was closer in age to me than my parents. I joked with some of my nurses that they should date Bama Boy, and they all agreed that he was good-looking. As soon as he arrived at the hospital every morning at 6:30 a.m., he came straight to my room. Asking me the same questions, he'd stick a camera up my nostrils and scope my nose. At the onset of any new symptoms or a rise in pain, he'd return to scope my nose.

All the while, my pain and pain-pump doses increased. I tried countless migraine medications, but nothing worked. Between the fungal pain and migraine pain, my doctors were doing me the favor of medicating me to the point of constant sleep. For weeks, my room remained pitch black, cold, and silent. I stepped out of bed only to go to the restroom and left my room only to go to the OR or for scans of my face.

During a two-week period, I had five surgeries to clean out the fungus. I was receiving IV antifungal and antibiotic medications around the clock. My blood levels were so low that my blood cells were not carrying the medicine to the infection to fight it off. The only way to get rid of the fungus was to physically remove it. I was also low on platelets, often too low to meet the requirements for surgery. Many times, my nurses would transfuse platelets quickly, only to send me down to the OR afterwards, with the freshly transfused platelets ready to try and help control the bleeding.

My face stayed packed with gauze for weeks, only to be unpacked with the daily nasal scopes and twice daily irrigations. The only way the doctors could tell if tissue was alive or dead was to prod it until it bled. I was almost relieved on the days I had surgery, as it meant a pass on the scopes and irrigations that night. The pain was always present, and the scopes only amplified it.

I was still not eating much but drank ice water constantly. As a child, I'd always requested water with no ice, as I am not a fan of cold water and prefer it at room temperature. But the pain was so bad that I sipped ice water in hope of relief. I was also trying to drown out the taste of blood. It was as if I could taste death, and the smell of blood combined with menthol in the ointment packed into my nose was a constant reminder.

Even when my fever spiked and my body was fighting fits of chills, I still requested ice water. When I was not allowed to drink anything before sedation but needed to take Tylenol for a fever, I would take a huge swig of my ice water and savor every bit.

They removed parts of my nose during those surgeries, so technically I had five nose jobs over the course of two weeks. While the last thing we were concerned about was what my face would look like, my nose surprisingly doesn't appear any different. Plastics even came in and placed a ruler on my face and evaluated, in case reconstruction would be necessary later. Luckily, it was not.

Plastics and ENT were not the only specialists to visit me daily. Optometry and Infectious Disease also joined my team, as well as all of the oncologists at the hospital. Optometry came by my room daily after ENT.

Bless that poor eye doctor's heart, he kept having me perform an eye test, except he used the same chart every single day. I tried to explain to him that I knew the chart by heart, but that only flustered him.

One morning, when he returned with his same chart, I said, "It isn't an accurate test." I closed both eyes and recited the letters.

It seems it would have been simple for him to bring a different chart for me to read, but for whatever reason, he never did. Finally, he put the chart away, but began a test that required physically touching my eye. When Mother and my team found out he had performed the test with my low platelet count, he was instructed not to do the test again. This was a reminder that no matter how engaged the team was, there was always a potential threat that could slip through and that just because there's a doctor in the room doesn't mean they're always right. I felt bad for him, because he was young and had not yet learned how to adapt to patients' varying circumstances.

Because my blood levels were low, I was receiving several Neupogen shots a day around 10 a.m. with hopes of boosting my counts. My arms and legs were covered in bruises, and my nurses struggled to find real estate on my body that was not blue and purple so that they could give me more shots. Years later, there is still a spot on my left thigh that is tinted brown, where a bruise from these constant shots stained my skin.

The brutal daily routine of tests, scopes, and cleanings was exhausting in and of itself. The migraines and fungal infection only amplified my pain and exhaustion. This was the first time that I have ever rated my pain a ten out of ten on the pain scale. Even when a tumor was growing inside me—the worst pain I had experienced before this—or when I considered any pain related to my Ewing's treatment, I had never said my pain was higher than an eight. Now, I wanted to shout that my pain was twenty out of ten.

39

As my body struggled to fight the fungal infection, it seemed as if so many of my nurses were not only pregnant, but approaching their due dates. Hannah, pregnant with her first child and just days away from birth, would squat down next to my bedside chair to help me do my daily irrigations and give me my daily shots.

Another nurse, Lauren E., who had been a favorite nurse since the beginning of treatment, was a month away from her due date. I had her three days in a row, with Halloween in the middle. She and several of the other nurses had dressed in costume as troll dolls in honor of the new *Trolls* movie release. They all had crazy colored hair and bright tutus: Amberly in pink, Ash-Leigh and Summer in purple, Hannah in green, and Krystle in red. I remember their costumes vividly because they were far more than just my nurses, they were my friends and support system.

As Lauren E. stood by my hospital bed and adjusted my IV pumps, Daddy and I asked her about the baby and if she was ready. She laughed and told us she did not even have a crib.

For Halloween, Mother and Bre had picked me out a Wonder Woman T-shirt, arm cuffs, and headband. I wore it all day, even in pre-op, as I had yet another nasal surgery on Halloween day. It was a tiny sliver of normalcy in my life when every second was consumed by the world of cancer, tiptoeing between consciousness and unconsciousness.

The day after Halloween, I was in really rough shape, and Lauren E. was also assigned to a second sick kid. The other patient and I kept Lauren E. on her feet all day. That night, my nurse, Victoria, told me that Lauren E. had gone into labor. She gave birth to a baby boy nearly a month early. Praise God, he was healthy. To this day, there are still jokes about how I sent Lauren E. into labor.

As much as possible, I just tried to sleep through the days. Infectious disease doctors visited regularly, telling my parents that the fungal infection was extremely close to both my left eye and my brain. If it were to spread to my left eye, I would lose vision in it. Worse, if it were to spread to my brain, I would be brain dead. My parents stayed by my side around the clock as my condition worsened. While I knew I was sick, I was not conscious enough to realize how close I was to the brink.

My nurses realized though. My parents would later talk

about how they began distancing themselves. If they were not assigned to care for me, they avoided my room. I was on my deathbed.

My friends also noticed that I was far sicker than I had ever been. While many friends always made efforts to visit me in the hospital, it seemed as if visitors were stopping by around the clock. Friends came to sit with me, pray with me, and quietly say goodbye to me.

On top of the looming threats of the fungal infection, there was an urgent time crunch. The only way I could get to my stem cell transplant was if we got rid of every bit of the fungal infection. I desperately needed a transplant. Transplant was my only cure, and at that point, it had become a big question mark.

Because of the migraines, I had several head MRIs. We needed to constantly watch and make sure the fungal infection was not spreading to my brain. Before this, MRIs did not make me feel claustrophobic, but with constant head MRIs—having to lie still with my head inside a box, inside of a loud tube that wrapped around my body—I grew anxious. I struggled to remain still. My team suggested the comfort of sedation, but because my blood pressure and heart rate were so off and all of my numbers so bad, the sedation team was hesitant. Katherine, my nurse practitioner, begged them to come by my room and visit me in person. The crazy thing was, despite how awful I looked and felt, and how awful I was doing, the numbers reflecting my condition painted a picture that was even worse.

Katherine pointed out that the "patient in the bed is not always the patient on paper" and succeeded in convincing the team to sedate me for my head MRIs.

One evening, my nurse promised Mother she would keep a close eye on me so that Mother could get takeout. While she was gone, things got shaky. My blood pressure was extremely low, and my heart rate was elevated. This can be a sign of going septic, a life-threatening infection in the blood, so my nurses had to call the STAT team, the Pediatric ICU team that comes to evaluate if a patient needs to transfer to the PICU. I did not feel great but also did not feel any worse than I had for weeks. I had a mild appetite and was well enough to have the lights on and to call Mother when things got rocky. She picked up after two rings. My voice was not firm, and I was nervous, but I knew I needed her. I managed, "Momma, my pressures are off . . ."

"Is it your blood pressure and heart rate?" I could hear the urgency in her voice.

"Yes, my blood pressure is low, and my heart rate is rising. I'm okay though."

I could hear rattling and guessed she was moving quickly. "Okay, I'm in the parking lot and heading up. I'll be there in just one minute. You're okay. It's going to be okay."

"I know," I reaffirmed confidently. "I don't even feel that bad," I lied. "They're calling for the STAT team though. Everyone is freaking out." I did not want to go to PICU and wanted to prove I was fine, but I knew it was serious if they were calling for the STAT team.

"I'm almost there. You're okay." I could hear her voice slow down as she was trying to remain calm and keep me calm—another giveaway that this was serious.

Mother arrived alongside the STAT team, her hands loaded with takeout bags. She had ordered several different foods in hopes that something might please my appetite.

After a quick evaluation, the STAT team made the decision to transfer me to PICU. I was disappointed and fought them tooth and nail. Despite the bargaining I attempted, they had no choice but to transfer me because my pressures were so off. The only progress I made was getting the team to allow me to get out of bed and use the restroom before being transferred to a PICU room where the toilet would be in the open with no stall. Four people, including Mother, hovered around me with their hands holding me up as I inched toward the bathroom. It's good I'm not that modest because in the hospital, modesty goes out the window.

I was distraught that I was being transferred to PICU. When Mother called Daddy to let him know what was going on, he said he knew I would be alright when he heard me in the background hollering to him about how I absolutely did not want to be transferred. As I was wheeled off the unit, I sat straight up on my bed and scowled at everyone. 4K was my home, not PICU. Maybe I was worried, on some level, that I would enter those PICU doors and never leave. While I knew everyone was only doing what they believed was best, I felt confident I was fine.

I was right. I was not septic, only dehydrated. By the time I was settled in at PICU, my levels had evened out. They kept me for the night and half the next day for observation. While PICU was not as bad as I expected and the nurses were extremely kind there too, it was still a fishbowl room with windows all around, bright lights, and loud beeps. Nurses are assigned one-to-one patient ratios, and mine was in my room all night. The noises, lights, and interruptions caused a lack of sleep that triggered a migraine, which meant an extra nasal scope. Anyone who has ever had a migraine would understand why that is not a time when you want to have a camera stuck up your nose until it bleeds.

Finally, I was transferred back to 4K. It was such a relief to be back, not only because of its familiarity, but also because it settled my fear that I would not return.

During the days of surgery, I would often go to the OR in the late afternoon. The OR usually schedules patients by age in the pediatric world, since patients have to be NPO and cannot eat or drink the day of surgery, the idea being that older kids can tolerate it longer. Being at the top of the age bracket, I was usually last. This meant that on top of everything else, I was not allowed to eat, despite the fact that we were working on growing my appetite.

Dr. Green-Murphy and Dr. Douglas would often spend time with me in the late afternoons and early evenings when they reached a stopping point for the day. Dr. Green-Murphy sat and listened to my concerns, worries, and fears. She helped me understand what was going on and entertained me when I was down.

Dr. Douglas was also a fellow, but he had spent many years as a pediatrician and decided to return for a fellowship to become a pediatric oncologist. He had spent some time in Nashville studying, and he told me all about it. I was hopeful that I was headed there soon for transplant. He told me about the exact replica of the Parthenon that was directly across the street from my hospital in Centennial Park. This would later become a favorite place of mine to go when I wanted to get out of the apartment, as it was approved by my transplant team since it was outdoors.

Maddi surprised me again one day after surgery. What little hair I had grown back after Ewing's was half gone. Maddi offered to shave my head for me, and my nurse, Amber, brought in towels for me to lie on as Maddi shaved.

In the photo of Maddi shaving my hair, taken by Amber, my eyes are closed, my head is leaned back on my pillow, and my face is packed. The photo is so raw, but it captures what my days looked like during one of the hardest points in the fight.

40

As I began to have moments of feeling better, Daddy offered once again to let me shave his head. He wanted to keep up the tradition of shaving his head as a nod to me and my fight. The day I said I finally had enough energy to do it, Tiffany was my nurse, and she filmed a Facebook Live video as I shaved off Daddy's curls. Filming a Facebook Live video reminded me of the real world outside of the hospital.

One day, as Mother was pushing me in my wheelchair from another CT scan back to my room, I told her I wanted KFC. Ordering takeout also kept me in touch with the world outside the hospital walls. While KFC is not typically a favorite of mine, I had decided that mashed potatoes and gravy sounded good. Mother was ecstatic that I had an appetite for anything. PaPaw was on his way to visit and stopped to pick it up. For two weeks, I would eat only a couple of bites of mashed potatoes with brown gravy a day. My parents and PaPaw would keep my mini fridge stocked with it. Eventually, I began adding a side of chopped peaches from the cafeteria. While I was not eating enough to get decent nutrition, it was a start.

A couple of days later, I asked Daddy to bring me Taco Bell, another fast food joint that is not my favorite but sounded good at the time. Daddy was so excited that he brought me back one of everything, as I was having trouble deciding what I would actually eat. While I only had a few bites of the tacos, it was a few more bites than I had been eating. It was progress.

I think it was so difficult to start eating again not only because my body already lacked an appetite, but also because it remained satisfied with my IV nutrition. Pediatric doctors are often quick to start IV nutrition, given the nature of their patients. But it kept me from having hunger pangs, making it more difficult to eat. That is why I have since made a strong effort to avoid getting nutrition by IV. I might even be guilty of minimizing my lack of appetite at times to keep doctors from starting the IV nutrition. I don't feel bad about it though, because every time I avoided it, I was able to get my appetite back on track all by myself.

We eventually learned that the fungal infection was a type called Curvularia. One day, a petite woman with a ponytail full of dark, wavy hair entered my room. I had no clue who she was but could tell by her attire and mannerisms that she was a doctor.

When I opened my eyes, she was looking right at me. She gasped, "You're awake!"

I must have looked confused because I didn't recognize her.

"I'm with infectious disease, and I have been monitoring your case. To see you awake is a huge step. I never get to see my patients awake."

I grinned as I processed her words.

"This must be a good sign that you are making a turn for the better. I usually keep chocolates in my desk and eat them when I get worried about my patients. I have eaten a lot of chocolates for you."

"Oh goodness. Well, thank you for everything you've done. It's nice to meet you."

The conversation was short, but it reaffirmed that a lot of doctors were monitoring and caring for me, even if I didn't know each of them. I never saw the woman again, but I am grateful for her.

I had been on a morphine pump for nearly two months. As we weaned it, I got sick. It took us a couple of days to realize the correlation to my sweats, nausea, vomiting, and chills. My nurse, Robin, figured it out. My body was going through withdrawal. It had gotten comfortable with the pain medicine and was deprived now. This is when I started methadone, the same medicine that is given to drug addicts to relieve withdrawal symptoms without creating an addiction. How embarrassing it felt to be taking methadone. The worst part though? The dose I was prescribed did not come in pill form. Not only was I taking methadone, but liquid methadone. A word to the wise, liquid methadone tastes awful. Chocolate helps.

As the methadone became part of my daily routine, I couldn't help but remember a comment from Katherine, my nurse practitioner, from one of the early days of treatment for Ewing's. She said, "We'll do what we have to do to get you better and keep you comfortable. If we have to wheel you out of here and straight into rehab, then we'll do that too."

It seemed so crazy when she first spoke those words, so unlikely that it could get that bad. Yet, here I was. Despite it all, I was appreciative that my team was willing to keep me comfortable. As hard as the withdrawals were, they were just part of the price I had to pay for comfort. I would have done anything to stop the kind of pain I had experienced, and the withdrawals seemed like a fair price to pay.

Imagine the movie scene from *When A Man Loves A Woman*, when Meg Ryan's character goes to rehab and experiences withdrawal, except worse because I had a list of underlying physical pains as well. It was rough, but methadone gets the job done, and it gradually provided relief.

What was supposed to be one month in the hospital turned into two months. We were all preparing to go to Tennessee, in hopes of a cure. I was making great strides toward healing from the fungal infection, but it did not get better overnight, and it was messy. I was still on daily IV medications to try and keep the infection at bay, still getting daily shots and irrigating my nose. Multiple blood and platelet transfusions were given to me every day.

Eventually, things began to improve. The surgeries were successful. The surgeons had removed all of the fungal infection. Finally, the surgeries stopped, but the scopes and cleanouts continued long after. It would still be another month before my nose would heal from the infection, surgeries, and constant scopes, and at least a year before I could sneeze or blow my nose without pain or blood. My face had to stay packed for weeks, and we couldn't be completely sure that all the fungus was gone. I healed slowly, but at least I was moving in the right direction.

The week of Thanksgiving rolled around, and I desperately wanted to go home. I had been gone for so long, and I was about to go even farther away to Tennessee. Due to my IV medications, I could not go home overnight.

A thoughtful family friend and her husband offered their Little Rock guesthouse to my family during the week of Thanksgiving. My entire family spent the week there, and I was able to join them at the little guesthouse when I received my first day pass on Thanksgiving Day. I took oral Ativan to keep up with my schedule from the hospital.

Mother cooked a feast for the six of us. We watched the Macy's Thanksgiving Day Parade and the annual Thanksgiving National Dog Show. We played games and decorated Christmas cookies. We were not at home, but we were together and out of the hospital. That is all I could ask for. Thanks to the couple who generously offered their guesthouse, the holiday was cheerful despite it all.

At the end of the day, I had to return to the hospital and hook back up to my IV pole for nightly infusions. I was given day passes the following two days to try and enjoy my time before going to Tennessee. I spent those two days with family and friends, got to see Pandora whom I had not seen in months, and even got to go out for dinner at Cantina Laredo, a favorite Mexican restaurant.

I sat in a dark booth in the corner. It almost didn't feel real. Physically, I was in the outside world, but the outside world had no clue that this was a momentary escape. After dinner, I walked down the sidewalk to ULTA. I peered through the window, watching a girl about my age. As she compared mascaras, I wondered, for just a moment, if that is what my life would look like had I not gotten sick again. I had forgotten what life was like outside of the hospital and all of the medications. To me, that life did not exist.

We left Little Rock at 5 a.m. on a Monday morning with hopes of making my 1 p.m. appointment in Tennessee. I knew I would be gone for a while, and, similar to when I'd been wheeled to the PICU, I questioned if I'd ever return. My nurses gathered in the hall to say goodbye. Some wrote me letters, others prayed, and all hugged. After a final 4K photo, Mother and Daddy loaded me up in Daddy's truck, and we headed northeast.

On the six-hour drive from Arkansas Children's Hospital in Little Rock to Tristar Centennial Children's Hospital in Nashville, Tennessee, I noticed the farther we drove, the fewer leaves we saw on the trees lining the highway.

I was extremely weak and sick. My teams were concerned about the lapse in time away from the hospital while traveling and had given my parents detailed instructions on how to handle potential scenarios. I believe my doctors must have had a great amount of trust in my parents to let them drive me to Tennessee.

On Daddy's truck dashboard, the temperature was dropping digit by digit. Then, it started to rain. I could hear the raindrops hitting the shell of the truck, thumping loudly. I felt sad to be leaving and going to this new place, even if there was a chance of finding a cure. I was leaving everything I knew and felt comfortable with. The rain seemed to set the tone for the dreariness. When the thuds stopped for a few seconds as we crossed under a bridge, I couldn't help but think about how the bad news had stopped for what felt like just a couple seconds between beating Ewing's and getting leukemia. Then the hard days picked right back up. I knew I needed to get better. I needed the transplant. *Maybe it won't be so bad*, I thought. *Maybe the rain means this is a fresh start.*

It was my first time visiting Tennessee, but there was no time for attractions since we had to go straight to the hospital for admission. As we made our way to the waiting room, we quickly realized that it was for multiple pediatric clinics, not just oncology. This meant that there were kids waiting in the same room for a variety of health concerns, some of them with contagious diseases. This was markedly different from ACH, where the waiting room I always sat in had *only* oncology patients. Even among the cancer kids at ACH, if any of us did catch something contagious, we were instantly isolated from other patients. With my weakened immune system, this every-one-in-one-spot situation felt very dangerous.

I did not know much about Dr. Haydar Frangoul prior to meeting him, but my family and doctors in Arkansas had done extensive research on him and communicated with him prior to the trip. A ball of friendly energy, Dr. Frangoul is short and has a slick bald head like his patients. Glasses rest on his tan face.

Through a thick Lebanese accent, he spoke quickly, sharing medical terminology that was difficult to grasp. But he took time to explain everything until I understood and all of my questions were answered. That first conversation left me with mixed feelings. He was extremely welcoming but also extremely honest.

After the greetings and formalities, he explained, "We are going to run some scans tomorrow to make sure everything is good before we move forward with treatment. We have a few options, but if we see anything, we will have to send you home."

The plan didn't completely sink in with me, but my parents understood that he was going to do a scan to see if there was any fungus, and if there was, there would be nothing he could do for me. While I heard his words "send you home," I misunderstood him to mean we would be scanning to see if there were any traces of Ewing's. I was confident there was no Ewing's. I would not have been so confident had I known we were scanning for Curvularia.

I was admitted to Centennial. I met the rest of my team including Dr. Domm, Katie (pharmacist), Julie (nursing and patient care coordinator), and Misty (transplant nurse practitioner). All four of these women are incredibly smart and have taken care of me over the last few years. Misty, in particular, stands out. Misty has her doctorate in nursing and teaches at Vanderbilt. She knows transplant inside and out. She is bilingual in a sense, able to speak the language of both doctor and patient.

I was shocked to find that the pediatric oncology and transplant patients stay on a general pediatric unit. Some milder cases were surgery patients for injuries like broken arms, but there were also babies with RSV and kids with the flu staying on the same hallway with cancer kids. This terrified me. I had spent my entire treatment experience distancing myself from these very things in order to protect my health, and now only a hallway separated me from all my greatest fears. This proximity scared me far more than any cancer diagnosis or treatment plan ever had.

To make light of the situation, we joked about the cat artwork in my outdated hospital room. To put it lightly, I am not fond of cats. While it has gotten much better with age, I am, and always have been, scared of cats. It is a real phobia, called ailurophobia. No offense to cat lovers, but they remind me of the devil and they always seem to be naughty and mischievous. So, to top everything off, there was cat-themed artwork hanging in my room.

Prior to transferring to my transplant hospital, I had heard transplant rumors through the oncology grapevine. Other patients, parents, nurses, and doctors shared stories of how transplant units are far stricter than regular oncology units. I'd heard stories that takeout was prohibited and ice from an ice machine would not be allowed. It sounded like I would have to bathe every couple of hours, visitors would not be allowed, my parents could potentially not be able to stay in the room, and when my parents did visit, they would have to enter through a scrub room where they'd wash their hands and arms before double gowning and gloving.

In contrast to what I had heard, I transferred to an older, general pediatric unit. My sheets were only changed when I requested it, and nobody charted whether I had showered that day or not. From what I could tell, the stories I'd heard are accurate at many pediatric transplant units, just not this one.

At the time, I could not understand why Dr. Frangoul would give transplants in such a situation. He said that when he moved from Vanderbilt to Centennial, he did not want to wait to start curing kids with transplants before they could build a new unit specifically for transplant, so he began transplants at Centennial before the unit was ready. He assured me that he could do transplants in his sleep. It turns out that research does not support the need for all of the rules I had been led to believe are necessary. I questioned Dr. Frangoul's methods often, but he was always able to back what he was doing with facts, research, and statistics. I kept a notebook specifically for points I wanted to discuss with him each day. He always responded well to my continued lists of questions and encouraged me to keep asking. When he entered my room, he would often jokingly begin our conversation by asking, "Where's the notebook?" He wanted me to be educated and involved in the decision-making process for my own health. Reflecting, I am eternally grateful that he went ahead and built his new program, otherwise I would not have been able to go to him when I needed him.

I trusted my team, but it was tough. I like rules. Rules make me feel safe. Rules provide comfort. I had relied on the idea that there would be more rules, and suddenly the rules I had at ACH did not even apply.

The nurses were new and the way they did things was different. I had several awesome nurses who helped bridge me between days with less-than-mediocre nurses, a few of whom did not like my questions and requests. This was a huge contrast to my nurses at ACH, who always encouraged me to ask questions and speak up when uncomfortable. It took me a while to adapt at Centennial, but I never stopped asking questions and advocating for myself.

I was still extremely sick, uncomfortable in my environment, and the farthest I had ever been from home (500 miles to be exact) for any extended period. There were a lot of tears. Dr. Frangoul did make some treatment modifications that I was a fan of, though. He switched me to a methadone dose that was compatible with oral pills instead of liquid. He also switched me to a different antifungal IV medication. Once I was ready to leave the hospital, I would be able to infuse it every night at the apartment my parents had rented just two miles from the hospital. Renting hotel rooms was adding up quickly, so they'd decided to sign a lease.

42

Around that time, Naina visited. She drove down from Chicago for an overnight stay and brought all of her planning supplies. It took a luggage cart to bring them in, and we spent the entire night munching candy, eating burgers from Red Robin, and planning. The afternoon she was taking her supplies to her car so she could head home, she shared she'd noticed another hospital room door on the floor that was heavily decorated. Knowing I always took pride in having my door and room decorated, she rushed into my room and excitedly informed me that there was competition. I laughed it off at first, but decided to mask and glove and go down the hall to see for myself.

Confronted by a door with a 3D fireplace constructed of cardboard, I rushed back to my room and immediately called Mother, who had gone to the store to pick up some hospital essentials.

"There's competition. I need you to go to Michael's for

supplies!" I basically squealed into the phone.

"What do you mean?" She questioned with a laugh.

"Naina saw this 3D chimney with Santa on another kid's door. We have to figure out a way to decorate my door BETTER!"

She was laughing hysterically, and I could hear Daddy chuckling in the background.

Without hesitation she asked, "What kind of supplies do you think we need?"

"I'm not sure . . . I don't really have a plan." I knew we didn't need a plan, though, because Mother is crafty and resourceful.

"Ok, I'll head that way before coming back to the hospital. What if I just FaceTime you when I get to Michael's and we go from there?"

"That sounds GREAT! Naina and I will brainstorm while we wait for you."

Naina was laughing the whole time. When I ended the conversation with Mother, Naina and I decided we'd decorate a tree with gift boxes below. The gifts would have my team members' names on them. From there, Mother and Daddy gathered supplies and did the work of decorating. I simply posed for a picture by the door and boasted to all of the nurses. I never did meet the kid behind the fireplace door, but he gave me something to look forward to on that gloomy day in the hospital.

43

Before transferring to Tennessee, I had only done one round of chemo to treat the leukemia. The fungal infection had delayed treatment so much that progress had not been made. Dr. Frangoul wanted to try a chemo called Decitabine. Often used in adult care, it causes few symptoms (in contrast to the chemos I had previously taken).

Once I completed a round of Decitabine, Dr. Frangoul agreed I could transfer to the apartment with my parents. The night before they moved in, they both decided to stay in the hospital room with me. To our surprise, unlike at ACH, which offered all the comforts my parents needed to sleep over each night, there were no extra recliners or vacant rooms we could borrow a recliner from. The nurses were not able to provide any solution as to where Daddy would sleep. This was peculiar and unexpected. Daddy made a palette of old hospital sheets and curled up in what little floor space my hospital room provided. It was very *Wizard of Oz*: "I'm not in Arkansas anymore."

Mother and Daddy were excited to get the apartment, and a few days later, I was able to join them. When it finally came time to discharge, Julie showed me how to take care of my line. While I had the line placed over two months prior, I hadn't been required to keep up with the maintenance on my own because I'd been in the hospital the entire time, where my nurses had done all of the work. Julie showed me how to check for blood return, flush both lumens—the tubes connected to my chest—with heparin, and hook up IV medications outside the hospital.

My line was different from the ports I had before. While there are pros and cons to both, I prefer the line. Both have a high infection risk, but the line is riskier. The line requires daily maintenance, whereas the port only needs to be accessed and flushed monthly. The line is a tube that hangs from your chest until surgically removed and requires weekly dressing changes, as well as changes anytime the dressing gets wet. This makes showers incredibly challenging. Ports can infiltrate easily, the infusion leaking into the surrounding tissue and causing pain, burns, itching, swelling, and an array of other symptoms. This can be particularly dangerous when receiving vesicants, or drugs that burn, into which category most chemos fall. Leaking happened to me several times, like the night I planned a New Year's party back at ACH. The ultimate factor for me, though, is that my first two ports flipped inside my chest, making them impossible to access. Both times, this resulted in immediate surgery before being able to replace the port and resume treatment. My line treated me at least slightly better.

I was happy that I'd be leaving the hospital and sleeping in a normal bed. I would have to go to clinic five or six days a week and would be on a strict schedule of both oral and IV medications around the clock, but being able to stay at the apartment was a slight taste of freedom that I was craving badly.

Mother had made a quick trip home to watch Bre in her State Cheer Competition, so it was just Daddy and me when I first left the hospital. I requested to stop at Sonic on our way to the apartment to try the new ice cream custard concretes. I barely ate a third of my small ice cream, but it was a nice treat to be able to drive through. Then, Daddy drove me through Centennial Park, right next to the hospital. The sun had just set, making the Christmas lights glow bright into the dark night.

When we arrived at the apartment, Daddy gave me a tour. They were proud of the place they'd found on short notice, and I was grateful for somewhere to call home, even if it was far from my real one.

During the few days between transferring to the apartment and waiting for the rest of my family to join Daddy and me, Mother suggested that I design new T-shirts for my transplant. I designed a "Nashville to Nashville" shirt, shared the link on Facebook, and when I woke the following morning, was surprised to find that I had already exceeded my goal. Between my hometown community and my online planner community sharing the link on Facebook, there were hundreds of shirt sales. Friends from home and around the country had placed orders. I was reminded that despite physically being far from all I knew and loved, thanks to technology, my loved ones were near.

Forty-eight hours later, Mother, PaPaw, Bre, and Andrew made the eight-hour trek from Nashville to Nashville for Christmas break. Mother's car and PaPaw's truck were loaded down with winter clothes, Christmas gifts, a tree, and decorations for the apartment. They arrived on my 19th birthday, December 18. Daddy had picked up a birthday cake shaped and iced like a furry little dog, which I'd chosen for its cuteness. It ended up being a bit morbid as we cut into the cake, reminiscent of the armadillo groom's cake in *Steel Magnolias*. I was less than interested in eating and felt pressured to pick our dinner meal when my appetite was absent.

I procrastinated deciding on dinner by opening my mail until it was nearly too late to order anything. I could tell that my family was growing hungry and trying to hide their impatience, so I eventually chose pizza. I barely had two bites.

I was also surprised with a thoughtful gift from Maddi. She had reached out to dozens of my friends, even my hospital friends she'd never met, to make a video collage of everyone wishing me a happy birthday. My struggles with homesickness were growing deeper. Yet this video surprise was comforting, reminding me of how many friends I had supporting me.

PaPaw surprised me with a thick coat, as the winter was unseasonably cold for the South. The following morning, I bundled up in my new coat and headed to clinic with Daddy. Pa-Paw, Mother, and Daddy must have each warned me a dozen times to watch for the ice patch on the sidewalk outside the apartment. I didn't hear one word though. While Daddy locked up, I stepped outside ahead of him and rounded the corner. As the sidewalk slanted downhill, I stepped toward the rail. The next thing I knew, I was on the ground, hollering for Daddy. He came running around the corner and picked me up, limping me along to get back inside.

I probably heard the words "I told you to watch for the ice patch" three times for each warning I had previously received. Because my body was eating up my daily blood and platelet transfusions instead of making more cells, my knees were severely bruised. I was sore for a few days, but it made for a good laugh later.

44

Christmas in Tennessee was not Christmas at home. I know that what matters is being with family, which I will be forever grateful for, but when you're in treatment and away from home, there is an ever-looming shadow, a pervading sadness that all is not well. There is the silent wondering if this Christmas will be the last. I pray to God that I never spend another Christmas away from home and sick, but I would still spend every Christmas like that if it meant more Christmases.

One of the hardest parts of being sick and away during the holidays was missing my friends. My family did a good job trying to cheer me up, but I felt lonely. I tried to counter it through FaceTime and Snapchat. And although I was away, my friends still found ways to show support. My friends Erica and Anna each had creative ideas to rally our community. Erica designed and sold "Kaden" shirts, and Anna gathered friends to make ornaments to sell as a fundraiser. It felt good to have support from so many friends during the worst days.

On Christmas Eve, I didn't want to go to the hospital, even if it was just for a few hours, but I had to. I needed a blood transfusion. The cherry on top was that I was assigned to a nurse who was not my favorite. She spoke to me with condescension and asked questions with a rude undertone. She just irked me. While on my best day, I could re-focus by telling myself that she probably didn't have bad intentions, but on that day, I didn't have the energy. This was my 100th blood transfusion, and I had anticipated making a post on social media when the day came, but I was so frustrated with the situation that I scrapped the idea.

PaPaw had gone home a few days before because his older brother was severely ill. Fred had lymphoma, a cancer of the lymph nodes, and was not doing well. PaPaw was waiting for me at the apartment when I got home at noon from my blood transfusion. After my morning of pouting, I was happy to see him.

During the holiday, he was torn by distance. His granddaughter and brother were both terribly ill. PaPaw had been able to go home to see Fred in the days leading up to Fred's death but was in Tennessee with me on the day he died. If I put myself in his shoes, PaPaw had it far worse than me that day.

It had always been easy to remain grounded during my first diagnosis, but when I moved to Tennessee, my emotions were like a hurricane of negativity. Only those who were in Tennessee with me and a few close friends and family members know how much I struggled emotionally and mentally during that time, as I often hid it with a smile, but this was the start of the darkest period I have lived through.

Due to the risks posed by germs, most places I was allowed to visit were outdoors. I could go to any restaurant with outdoor seating, as well as parks and festivals. But this was a challenge in December, when hardly any restaurants had outdoor seating and there were not many events outdoors. When we did find a place outside, I could only stay briefly because of the cold.

My siblings spent their Christmas break with me in Tennessee. I recall a few times when they encouraged me to get out of the apartment. Mother and Daddy drove us to look at Christmas lights or around town.

Occasionally, I would sneak into Sephora or the Kate Spade store right after they opened or just before closing in order to avoid crowds. A couple of my favorite memories in Tennessee involve going to Nordstrom Rack to browse the Kate Spade purses, eating a steak quesadilla at Uncle Julio's across the street, and ending the evening with Jenni's Splendid Ice Cream.

One evening during Christmas break, while I was admitted to the hospital, my family gathered around my hospital bed. In walked Maddi and her parents, Steve and Leslie. Maddi came bearing gifts for my birthday and Christmas, and her parents brought Mexican takeout. We visited for hours as Ativan and Benadryl pumped continuously into my veins.

Maddi and I asked Mother if just the two of us could have a sleepover. Mother agreed and stayed at the apartment just two miles away that night. This was one of two nights that I have ever spent in the hospital without family. That night, Maddi and I watched a random Netflix movie about a scandalous wedding. The plot was mediocre and Maddi fell asleep halfway through, but I went to sleep happy, despite being in Tennessee, in the hospital, receiving yet another blood transfusion.

The following morning, Maddi and I devoured Waffle House takeout, courtesy of Steve and Leslie. When Maddi had to go home, Daddy also had to take Bre and Andrew home, as Christmas break was ending. I cried when everyone left, and Mother sat in my hospital bed holding me as the shadow of sadness crept in. Luckily, in the following hour, as PaPaw pulled into the hospital parking lot, sunshine returned.

45

After two more rounds of chemo, there was still leukemia present in my marrow. Dr. Frangoul made the strategic decision to give me a chemo called Mylotarg. At the time, it was not approved by the FDA and had been pulled off the market due to being unsuccessful in treating leukemia. The conclusion had just recently been made that it actually was efficient and successful, and it was in the process of making its way back on the market. ACH had not been able to access it, but somehow, Dr. Frangoul had connections.

All of the nurses were excited about this mysterious drug, and I must admit it gave me a bit of a thrill to safely try something not approved by the FDA. It made me feel bad in a good way. PaPaw arrived just in time for my nurse to hang the bag on my IV pole. I recall trying to visit with him and falling asleep mid-conversation, due to the IV Benadryl I'd been given to combat the chemo's side effects.

Vomiting several times a day for months had become routine, almost as if my body was on autopilot. My team decided to try a new medicine, Zyprexa. The medicine's intended use is as an antipsychotic medication, but I was prescribed it to increase my appetite. The thought was, if I ate an insane amount of food, it didn't matter whether or not it all stayed down. At least I would still be getting some nutrients.

The appetite part of the plan worked. I ate 24/7, driven by a hunger within me that could not be sated. I would be eating a footlong sandwich from Subway and order a four-course meal before finishing. But Zyprexa made me crazy. My emotions were extremely unstable, and I cried constantly.

Every day, I would be weighed. As I watched the number on the scale creep up daily, I would curse my pharmacist's name. We had some laughs about my frustrations, but ultimately it was too much and we had to stop the medication. My mental health was already fragile, and this medication was only magnifying my struggles.

Before stopping Zyprexa, though, one of the greatest moments in my life occurred. I was sitting in my hospital room inhaling a plate of bacon, pancakes, sausage, and French toast sticks, when Misty, my nurse practitioner, entered my room. She greeted me with great news: the donor had agreed to donate stem cells, and I was going to receive what would be my first stem cell transplant. I was ecstatic. I excitedly questioned Misty to learn if it was really true, if they really agreed to donate. Through laughter and tears, she confirmed the news. I will never forget my joy as Mother squeezed me in a bear hug.

While waiting for my transplant date, my body only grew more desperate for a cure. Leukemia aside, my marrow was shot. I was not producing enough cells to make blood, and my body was eating up what few cells I was producing. I was having blood and platelet transfusions daily. I had over fifty-five transfusions during January and February, thirty percent of the transfusions I would have throughout the next four years of treatment.

Leading up to the transplant, my mental health continued to decline. I had not been home since before the leukemia diagnosis five months prior. I was miserable in Tennessee. My parents were taking shifts, and I struggled being away from the people in my life, especially Mother when she was home with my siblings. I wanted so badly to be happy but cried often in sorrow and anger. Daddy did not know how to respond, so he took me for milkshakes and tried to give me words of courage.

One night, I called Mother, hysterical. I hated where I was in life. "I just feel stuck here," I cried out to her.

She firmly responded, "You are not stuck. If you want to go home, you can. You are 18, almost 19. You're an adult. This decision is yours to make."

She knew that I wanted my transplant and would not make the decision to end treatment so that I could go home. Besides, she wouldn't have actually let me go home. This was just her way of encouraging me to keep moving forward. In the moment, I was furious with her.

I defeatedly responded, "This is my only option. I have to be here."

"Kaden . . ." her voice softened. "You are choosing to be there. You *get* to be there."

Everything felt out of my hands. I wanted to be in college like all of my friends. This is the one and only time that I hung up the phone before saying goodbye. I cried that whole night. The following morning, Daddy and I had a conversation. He is not a man of many words, but he encouraged me to call Mother, which I did, resulting in us quickly making up.

After Mother and I finished talking, Daddy and I headed to clinic. As I sat in the passenger seat of his truck, I peered out the window and watched rain drip down. It was always raining in Tennessee, and I was still feeling defeated. Then, through the truck speakers, I heard, "This is my FIGHT SONG, take back my LIFE SONG." I looked up toward the radio, recognizing the song I'd chosen for the wedding. I was instantly reminded of the promise Keagan and I made to each other and knew what I needed to do: Keep moving forward.

Getting this little sign during my slump also gave me the chance to sort through my feelings about what had happened with my mom. It isn't that I was truly considering going home. I was just miserable with the situation. She wasn't actually leaving the decision in my hands, even though it felt like it. I believe if I would have opted not to go forward with the transplant, she would have talked me out of that decision. Luckily, it didn't come to that, but she must have known the power of emphasizing to me that there is always a choice, even when it doesn't seem like it. This was Mother's way of reminding me of our shared perspective that there was a time to stop the tears and stand up strong. It worked.

I come from a long line of strong women. I believe it is alright to cry, but at some point, you have to stop crying and do something. While I was not excited about being in Tennessee or having a transplant, I never forgot for a second after that night the reason I was there: to get better, so I could go home and keep living.

From there, I had to continually make a conscious effort to remember that I was on God's time and that I was exactly where I *needed* to be, even if it wasn't where I *wanted* to be. My faith in Him rooted me through both the mental and physical challenges I faced. My time in Tennessee was a difficult sacrifice that I chose so that I could have a better quality of life. Or, as hard as it was to think about, to have life itself.

46

"Even if we were able to magically eliminate the leukemia, your bone marrow is depleted," Dr. Frangoul commented a few times during my daily clinic visits.

I was no longer producing new blood cells and was requiring multiple blood and platelet transfusions daily. The transfusions were simply buying time until we could transplant new marrow.

Flowing with intelligence, Dr. Frangoul was giving tons of information about the history and process of transplant in preparation for my own. During one of our many conversations, he talked about the bombing of Hiroshima and Nagasaki that killed many during World War II. The bombing played a key part in the study of radiobiology. Many of the lives lost were due to marrow being killed by radiation. My bone marrow was in a situation extremely similar to their bone marrow: dead.

There are two types of stem cell transplants, one called

autogenous and one called allogeneic. With auto transplants, doctors take the recipient's own stem cells, alter the cells, and return them to the recipient's body. In allo transplants, doctors take donor stem cells and transplant them into the recipient's body.

It is important to note that I use the terms "stem cell transplant" and "bone marrow transplant" interchangeably. Donors can give either bone marrow or peripheral stem cells, but both work for a transplant. A bone marrow transplant is a stem cell transplant, but a stem cell transplant is not necessarily a bone marrow transplant. If the donor gives peripherally, stem cells are pulled from the blood. If the donor gives through bone marrow, stem cells are pulled from the bone marrow. Either way, stem cells are given to the recipient through a central line in the chest, and the only difference is the number of days it takes to engraft. In both donations, the stem cells are used to build new bone marrow and stem cells in the recipient's body. Because the infusion process and results are the same, the terms "stem cell transplant" and "bone marrow transplant" are often used interchangeably in the transplant unit. These cells would be given to me peripherally, but all that meant was it took me a few more days to start engrafting—when the donor's cells make a home in the recipient's body and begin to build blood cells that would hopefully fight the leukemia cells.

My need for a transplant grew every day. When the week to

admit and begin the pre-transplant protocol approached, the plan we had charted was set into motion. Mother was at home with my siblings and was planning to return the day I was admitted for my pre-transplant protocol. Daddy was with me in Tennessee.

In the days leading up to my hospital admit, Daddy started coughing and then grew sicker. Since he was my caregiver, we were spending a great amount of time living in the apartment and riding in the car together. This was a serious situation, because it could be dangerous for me to have any kind of infection—even the common cold—as I entered transplant preparation. Once the preparation process begins, there is no stopping or postponing.

Typically, when we had illnesses growing up, we would just visit my grandpa, Sam. He would examine us and order antibiotics if necessary. Being eight hours away, that was not an option. Daddy did not have a doctor in Tennessee, and my doctors could not write him a script, since he was not their pediatric oncology patient.

At the last minute, we had to revise our plan. Mother bought a plane ticket to Tennessee and as soon as Daddy picked her up from the airport and dropped her off at the apartment, he hit the road. Because we were trying not to spread germs, I didn't even get to hug him goodbye. I could only wave.

Nonetheless, the dilemma was solved—or so we thought. I had about 48 hours until I was due to admit into the hospital and roughly 74 hours until pre-transplant treatment began.

Mother helped me pack my bags for another lengthy hospital stay and we spent time driving around the city before I would spend a month confined to one room.

The night prior to my transplant admission, we ordered Mexican takeout. We snuggled up on the couch and watched reality television while indulging in our last supper.

Not long after we went to bed, Mother became incredibly ill. I slipped Zofran and blue bags through the door as she mustered up the words to scold me for risking my health. We later learned that she likely was just sick from her food, but at the time it was not clear whether or not she had a stomach bug.

The following morning, she'd made no improvements. I was too weak to even consider driving myself to the hospital, and I didn't need to be close to her either. I called clinic and spoke to both Misty and Julie. Julie promised that they would find a way to get me to the hospital, even if someone had to drive to our apartment and pick me up. She instructed me to shower and get ready while they worked on a plan.

A bit later, I received a call from an unreliable clinic social worker I'd previously encountered. On the periodic occasions she was at work, she typically lacked the effort needed to be helpful. She called to get information on the situation and told me to get a cab. I immediately informed her that I would not take the health risks of riding in a cab where countless other people had been. She then suggested Uber, to which I responded the same. I guess she thought I did not have money for an Uber, so she explained that she could get me a voucher. I slowly explained that money was not the issue, but that the risk of germs pre-transplant was the concern. She was not much help from there and told me that somebody would call me back. No one did.

Several hours later, Mother and I realized that we were just going to have to take matters into our own hands. If you want something done right, sometimes you just have to do it yourself. Mother and I both masked and gloved and leaned as far away as possible from each other as she drove me to the hospital. It's a wonder that she made the drive without getting sick.

On Valentine's Day, Mother dropped me off at the front door of the hospital. I rolled my suitcase toward clinic.

Everyone was surprised to see I had made it, but my parents developing a common cold and stomach bug was not going to hold me back. I admitted and spent the one and only night I have ever spent by myself in the hospital.

It felt strange to be alone. At my hospital in Arkansas, I have close relationships with my nurses, but not as much at my Tennessee hospital. I spent the night eating a hamburger from the cafeteria and watching *Jersey Shore* reruns.

As odd as it felt, there is a part of me that feels guilty for only having one night in the hospital by myself. I know so many other pediatric patients, kids and teens both, who spend every night in the hospital without family. My family has gone out of the way to make sure at least one person, often two people, are always with me. It is more than a blessing, but rather an extreme privilege that my family is able and willing to take such great care of me.

The following morning, PaPaw was at the hospital first thing. He delivered Valentine's chocolates and candies from him and Daddy. I started pre-transplant chemo that day, which made me feel just crummy enough that I didn't want to eat them.

PaPaw also delivered my mail. As I opened it, I thought of other packages I had ordered. Online shopping helped because it gave me a little something exciting to look forward to. After unveiling a Kylie Jenner Lip Kit, I swatched the liquid lipstick on the back of my hand. When I was done testing it, I attempted to wipe it off with makeup remover, but struggled to remove it. The following day, my hand was still stained. The Kylie Jenner Lip Kit era was iconic because the lip kits were viral must-haves . . . but they wouldn't come off. Once people started buying them, they learned that they were super permanent and it would take at least a day or two to fully remove. For me, it did make for a fun distraction. I remember joking with Misty that despite not being able to remove the lipstick from my hand, I was keeping up with my hygiene.

Over the next few days, I began to experience pain so intense that it was hard to think of anything else. At first, I felt tingling, itching heat on my feet. Then they burned as if I were standing in fire. My breathing grew faster, and my heart rate rose. I was on a morphine pump and taking Oxy around the clock, yet my pain was still at an eight or nine.

Eventually, I was switched to a continuous Dilaudid pump to provide clarity to my medication schedule for a less-than-caring-and-efficient nurse. She carried her attitude in her voice and was huffy with me, coming across as if she was bothered to have to take the time for my care. It appeared as if it didn't matter to her whether I was in pain or crying.

We initially believed that the pain was being caused by the chemo, Busulfan, but would later discover that I had an adverse reaction to the immunosuppressant medication, Tacrolimus, which is what caused the itching and burning on my feet.

So much anticipation built toward the transplant that when the day finally arrived, it felt surreal. It was 9 a.m. when they brought in the cells. I jokingly instructed my team to slow down, as I had not finished applying my eyeliner and wasn't ready to be photographed. As they hooked me up to receive the infusion of stem cells that we hoped would save my life, I sat bundled in my fluffy robe, blending my eyeshadow. I had been warned by my team that the actual infusion process is the least eventful part of the entire transplant and the chaos would ensue in the coming weeks and months as my body adjusted to building a new, foreign bone marrow and immune system. They weren't wrong. It felt similar to a blood transfusion. I got a big dose of IV Benadryl to prevent any reactions, then the infusion began through my central line. Other than the high of the Benadryl, I felt nothing.

My siblings had arrived in time for the transplant infusion, and we found two ways to celebrate the occasion together. Just after transplant, Daddy picked up IHOP for everybody to eat in my hospital room. That afternoon, we had cake to celebrate my new birthday.

As my parents and Bre went to pick up dinner that night, Andrew played video games next to my bed and chatted with me. I was choking back tears from the pain in my feet. While Andrew didn't seem uncomfortable, it bothered me as the older sister that I might be revealing the pain I was in. I am supposed to be strong, yet I was hurting. Maybe at that point he was desensitized. It didn't seem to upset him to have to go get my nurse a couple of times. He just wanted to make sure I was alright. Whereas birth order might dictate that I should have comforted him, he comforted me.

Within the first couple of days after the transplant, the lining of my mouth and throat began to shed. While I remembered signing something listing this as a possible side effect, it felt peculiar to be confronted with the fact that my entire body was regenerating all new cells and disposing of the old. It was nasty and required a lot of suction. I stopped eating for a few days, and it hurt to swallow my pills. The 40 pills I was taking per day were hard enough to choke down with a sick stomach and weak appetite, but now it was causing me pain as well. We had to crush them and mix them with applesauce, and even that hurt to swallow. I can still remember the salty taste and gritty feel of those crushed pills, like baking soda and grainy sugar combined.

The Dilaudid made it difficult for me to stay awake long enough to finish a thought. PaPaw joked with me because I would often fall asleep sending him a text and then wake up and hit send after my fingers had hit a bunch of random keys on the keyboard.

All of my side effects were normal and expected until I began to display cold-like symptoms. My doctors wanted to X-ray my chest to eliminate the possibility that it was pneumonia. While we were waiting on the results, my mom ran into my nurse in the hallway. Mother asked if she had heard any results, and the nurse solemnly replied that I had pneumonia.

Mother returned to my room in a state of panic. We had been warned of this risk, and that it could be fatal if not treated properly. She immediately began working on a Facebook post to update and ask for prayers. My notifications were instantly flooded with prayers and well wishes as we sat in a state of shock.

The following morning during rounds, nobody mentioned pneumonia. When I brought it up, my team informed me that my lungs were not super clear, but I did not have pneumonia, only rhinovirus—the common cold. While this cold was still a threat to my health post-transplant, to say we were relieved is a massive understatement.

Years later, I am still in disbelief that a nurse told us results that were completely incorrect. I had the same nurse that following night, and she never said a word about the pneumonia fiasco.

48

One afternoon while recovering from my transplant, Bre and Mother went shopping for her prom dress while PaPaw sat with me. That night, Bre brought her dress to my hospital room and tried it on for me. It was a one-of-a-kind dress that was not traditionally styled, a black leather romper with a skirt around the back. Bre loved her dress so much that she wore it for hours while we watched a Britney Spears documentary.

Being on a general pediatric floor where there were all kinds of illnesses, I was not allowed to leave the room. Two days prior to my discharge, I was granted permission to leave the unit and step outside for some fresh air. Because I was over 18, a nurse did not have to go with me, only my parents.

As soon as the nurse unhooked me from the IV pole, I walked straight to the elevators, outside, through the parking lot, and to Daddy's truck without looking back. My parents had arranged for my dog, Pandora, to be there in hopes that it would cheer me up. I hopped in the truck to tail wags and squeals, and my parents drove me across the street for drive-through chicken tenders.

For the remainder of the break, we sat in Daddy's truck at Centennial Park. I relaxed in the backseat with the windows down and Pandora in my lap, appreciating every minute. Holding her and breathing some fresh air felt great after being stuck in the same hospital room for weeks. While I didn't do anything that put me at risk, I wasn't supposed to leave the hospital, so technically, I snuck out. It felt nice to take control for a short period of time and make the decision to do something for my mental health. Ativan could only take me so far and this break helped immensely. I returned when I was supposed to and my parents began loading my items up to take to the apartment.

When Dr. Frangoul came by to check on me that afternoon, he jokingly asked where all of my stuff had gone. I politely informed him that the plan to discharge in two days was happening no matter what. I like to be bold when setting my medical goals. It pushes both me and my doctors to move forward. It paid off too, because I was discharged as I planned and far earlier than expected prior to the transplant.

49

The first 100 days post-transplant are the most critical. I needed to be constantly monitored by my transplant team. After being discharged from the hospital, I moved into the apartment since I had to stay in Nashville and return to clinic daily for the bulk of the first 100 days.

I was still taking nearly 40 pills a day. My pharmacist, Katie, had explained to me that taking Oxy on a schedule around the clock would be an easy way to ease off the pain pump and hopefully avoid withdrawals again. It worked, and I only had to take scheduled Oxy for a couple weeks while staying in the apartment.

As I began to feel better, I was desperate to go home. My health was improving, and my parents began alternating shifts, one staying with me in Tennessee and the other with my siblings in Arkansas. I tried to fill my schedule with as much as possible.

I searched online and through Facebook for outdoor festivals in the city. We went to countless craft and music festivals. One of my favorites was the Japanese Cherry Blossom Festival, for its food, vendors, and entertainment. Food trucks with both traditional Japanese food and fair food circled a grassy patch where crowds of people surrounded singers and dancers.

I also spent a lot of my free time online. With an extension on my school work from the fall semester, there was plenty to wrap up. Window shopping on the internet became a regular activity. I loved comparing makeup and clothing from different sites and finding deals and steals.

During times that were not as busy, I was allowed to go to the mall and the movies. There were many mornings that I was standing by the door when Sephora opened. It was always comical when I needed wheelchair assistance and it was Daddy's turn to stay with me in Tennessee. He would kindly push me through the aisles of makeup and swatch shades of eyeshadow on his own hand so I would not touch the commonly touched and likely germy samples. Once, when Mother was staying with me, we went to Sephora, then ULTA, then back to Sephora—all in one day. When we went to the movies, I'd sneak in a bag of microwave popcorn and cover my theater seat with a blanket, both to avoid germs.

Finally, I was in the last month of my 100-day stint in Tennessee. Summer was around the corner, and I was able to start wearing shorts and sandals. One night, Daddy made tacos while I watched *The Real Housewives of New York City*. When I walked into the living room around 11 p.m to say goodnight, I showed Daddy a sunburn on the tops of my feet from where my skin was exposed around my sandals. I have always been extremely prone to sunburns and that was amplified from transplant. Sunburn was a huge concern, as it can trigger graft versus host disease. This could be problematic because of the risk of it causing pain at best and organ failure at worst. There was a balance of wanting the new cells to fight the leukemia but not my body. He was sitting in the recliner with Fancy, Mother's deaf dog. As I walked around the corner of the chair, I startled Fancy. She barked, which in return startled me. I jumped up in shock and landed wrong on my foot. I fell.

"It's broken!" I proclaimed, through tears of pain. My blood stained the carpet.

Daddy is usually calm, but I could tell by his lowered tone of voice that he knew this was another emergency. He quickly changed into clothes to take me to the emergency department. He wheeled my wheelchair over and tried to lift me into it. I couldn't bear any weight, and my good leg was not strong enough to solely support me.

Between the antics, I hysterically called Mother. She tried to calm me on the phone as Daddy ran around the apartment preparing to go to the hospital. As we were ready to leave, he stopped to get a bottle of water and asked me if I would like one as well.

"No, we need to go!" I said, feeling panicked. While he meant well, I was not interested in staying hydrated.

As Daddy was helping me to the car, he offered to go in his truck instead to avoid my car being covered in blood stains. I can be a clean freak, and I am particular about my car. I was so desperate to get to the hospital that I brushed it off and told him we could go in my car.

"When you were willing to risk blood stains," Daddy later said, "I realized how bad it was."

Daddy called my oncologist to alert them I was heading into the emergency department, so they could let the ED know to have a room ready to keep me from sitting in a germy waiting area. When we arrived, Daddy went inside first. The ED had not yet heard from my oncologist, but they were quick to prepare a room.

The doctor wrapped my foot and stopped the bleeding. An X-ray showed a fracture. I would need a boot and would be on crutches. By 4 a.m., we made it back to the apartment. Pain aside, the whole situation was so ridiculous it was actually comical. I still tease Daddy about the timing of his water bottle offer.

The following morning in clinic, I was fitted for the boot and crutches. I needed a medium, and they only had small and large. We tried stuffing the boot, but neither size was effectively working. This led to Daddy going on a hunt for an orthopedic store in the city. He was able to find one, and I am positive that he was charged double what a boot should cost, but he purchased it, as well as a shower chair for me.

The next week, I was granted a weekend trip home for Easter Sunday. As Daddy drove over the Memphis bridge that connects Tennessee and Arkansas, he cheerfully greeted me with, "Welcome back to Arkansas, Kaden!" This would become a tradition every time I crossed that bridge with him. Even on the couple of occasions I rode home with Mother or PaPaw, he called me from his truck to welcome me back home. Whether the trip had been for one night or one hundred, his welcoming was always a relief—a reassuring reminder that I had made it back.

Mother had decorated the entire house and planned a big meal for Sunday lunch. For two weeks, I'd looked forward to the trip home and all of the yummy foods she planned to cook. To top it all off, Andrew had completed confirmation class and made the decision to be baptized that Sunday. It was set to be a weekend full of celebration. But by the time I made it back home to Nashville, Arkansas, I was sick to my stomach. I spent all of Saturday in bed, hoping to be better for Sunday lunch. By Sunday, I was even worse. My stomach was empty, and I was dehydrated.

After calling Dr. Frangoul, we all decided that I needed to go into the emergency department at ACH in Little Rock. Andrew's baptism was still set, so we headed to the church. Andrew was baptized and a cake was cut, then Mother and I hit the road. At the ED, I was still in my Easter dress.

I was relieved to see my nurse Ashley, who crossed over between the oncology clinic and the emergency department. There is nothing like having a nurse who is familiar with you and has treated you before. It was also nice to catch up and visit. The last time I had seen her, I could barely hold my head up.

To top it off, Dr. Long, a fellow at the time, was making the rounds in the ED. I had been her patient when she made oncology rounds as a resident. She and the other resident making rounds with her that month, Dr. Freese, are the only two residents that have ever done an exceptional job at taking care of me. Most residents are fresh out of medical school and have not yet mastered thinking outside of the book for their patients. Dr. Long and Dr. Freese went beyond what the textbook said and treated me by my individual needs. Not only that, but they were fun to be around and went out of their way to make me smile. Sometimes unintentionally, residents can make treatment more difficult at times, but these two made mine easier.

Dr. Long decided to admit me for the night to receive fluids. We debated on just giving me fluids in the ED and discharging, but since I was headed back to Tennessee to finish out the final few days of the 100 and Little Rock is two hours into the trip, we admitted so I could rest while getting fluids.

The next morning, it was time to cross the bridge into Tennessee once more.

50

Once I returned home for good, I was ready to resume normal activities. That summer, I enrolled in classes for the fall semester at my local community college. I wanted to be able to continue working toward my bachelor's degree, but I was not quite physically ready to live by myself again.

During this time, I became a Make-A-Wish ambassador, attending fundraisers and representing kids and teens across the state as a former Wish kid. I also joined the Arkansas Children's Hospital's Circle of Friends, consisting of chapters throughout the state that raise funds for ACH. I learned about the Garland County chapter through my friend DeaAnn, who had given me a ride in the homecoming parade. She grew up in Nashville and moved to Hot Springs, only an hour away, where the Garland County chapter is located. Through her and the other chapter members, I had the opportunity to give back to the hospital that had been my home. We collected items so the hospital could provide teens with age-appropriate toy closets. We also started an annual fashion show in my hometown with the help of a close friend, Gail. One hundred percent of the fashion show's profit goes to the oncology unit at Children's.

This period at home was good for me. I was able to be close to family and friends, work on my strength, continue recovering, and even get some college hours knocked out. Eight months post-transplant, I began to feel stronger and eager to move out, but I had been told by my transplant team that it would likely be at least a year before I would have enough immunity to actually move out and go to school. Despite gaining stamina overall, we began to notice that my left leg was not healing like the rest of my body, and I was falling several times a week. I began seeing new doctors to try to figure out what was wrong with my leg.

I didn't have the ability to stand up after falling and relied on others to help lift me. I knew that if I wanted to be able to live on my own I would need to be capable of standing up after a fall without help from somebody else.

Max had been my physical therapist for over a year, and he always seemed eager to help me learn and develop new strengths. I decided to ask Max for help with learning how to stand up by myself after falling. I told him my plan to try to move out, and he was eager to help me reach my goal. We spent an entire therapy session practicing on a soft mat, and eventually I was able to stand up by myself.

As soon as I went home after physical therapy with my

new skill, I plopped down onto the floor in front of my parents and instructed them to watch as I stood up without any assistance. I then FaceTimed Maddi to show her.

I mentally checked the box on this first step to moving out. Next, I offered to cook dinner one night. I made a big pot of chili and an apple cobbler, wanting to show I could take care of myself. Then I subtly—or perhaps not so subtly—began hinting that I was ready to move out. Mother reminded me that my transplant team would need to approve it first.

In November, I was due for a checkup in Tennessee. I planned to ask my team for their blessing to move out on my own. During the drive, I quickly picked up that Daddy was hesitant. He wanted me to be able to, but he didn't want me to rush it before my body was ready. Before my leukemia diagnosis, I had only lived in a dorm for seven weeks. This would be different, as I was planning to move into an apartment, which seemed like a bigger life step. It became clear that Daddy was planning to make sure my team was confident this was the best choice for me. My doctors do not like to tell me no, and they want me to have the best quality of life possible. Sometimes this resulted in allowing me to do things that they maybe don't think are the best ideas. Daddy wanted this decision to be well thought out by everyone because if it didn't go well, we'd all have to live with the consequences.

When we arrived in clinic, I was prepared. I presented all of the reasons why I should be able to move out to my nurse practitioner, Misty. She listened carefully to me and then to Daddy as he politely expressed his concerns. When we had both pleaded our cases, I took a deep breath and asked for her opinion.

Misty nodded her head and said, "You're recovering exceptionally well. I feel like you're ready." While Daddy was still worried, he respected her opinion, and that was enough for him. It also probably helped that my Aunt Tammy and Uncle Keith lived in the same city where I would be transferring for school at the University of Central Arkansas. Tammy was like a mom away from home for me, which had to have comforted my parents.

It was nice to know that I would have my own place. I had long been craving that taste of freedom and normalcy, two feelings that had been stripped from me during treatment.

51

The day before I was set to move into my apartment, my Ewing's Sarcoma soul sister, Asher, died. Her mother, Susan, had been posting updates on Facebook, and Asher's health had been declining. I knew it was coming, but it was still hard. I thought of how she taught me to decorate my hospital room and of how many days we spent playing Barbies while receiving chemo and blood transfusions together.

Many other patient kids have inspired me over the years, but Asher will always stand out. She lived more life in those short nine years than many people live in 100. She inspired others not to let anything stop us and to make the best of the situation, however awful it may feel. It was hard to see somebody as astounding as Asher die, but her death left me even more motivated to conquer life in her memory as I pursued an education.

Two days before I started class, I woke up with my left

eye swollen shut, red, and itchy. I went in to see my oncology team in Arkansas, which referred me to the eye doctor that afternoon. While concerns of graft-versus-host disease or an eye infection were on the table, we determined it was cellulitis, the same skin infection that had caused me problems with my knee nearly two years prior. I was instructed to wash my eye several times daily and prescribed an antibiotic, but was released to start class the following day.

This was a problem. My eye was too red and swollen for eye makeup, let alone contacts. It is definitely *not* my style to go to class without makeup, especially on the first day.

It ended up working out, except for my school ID picture. I wore glasses, which was not my style preference, and behind the lenses, my eye was puffy. To make matters worse, I was self-conscious about my short, thin hair, and the employee taking my ID photo insisted that I take my hat off and was less than kind when I became emotional. This reminded me that I was transitioning from the cancer world, where people tended to understand and be empathetic, to the wider world, where strangers might not always show kindness.

Spring semester at UCA was great. I made friends, and we coined ourselves the "Salty Squad." I learned to meal prep and enjoyed apartment living with Pandora.

Between classes, I had many medical appointments. Every three months, I had post-Ewing's scans. Labs were drawn and vaccines were administered monthly because the transplant wiped out all of my vaccinations, requiring me to receive all of my shots again. On top of those appointments, I was traveling to Tennessee every six months for testing.

I scheduled an appointment with my gynecologist. All of the radiation and chemotherapy I had undergone posed a risk for my reproductive organs, despite my decision to have surgery to move my ovaries in an attempt to avoid any damage. After some testing, my gynecologist determined that my lab work indicated ovarian failure. While this sounds scary, it simply means that it will likely be difficult for me to have kids. The statistics don't look good, but I have seen God step in many times when medicine was working against me.

While I'm nowhere near ready to even think about having kids, I do like the idea of adopting one day. Mother was adopted, and I have seen the great joy she brings PaPaw. I grew up dreaming of potentially adopting a daughter as well one day. This development with my health simply shifted my mindset to viewing adoption as how I will have children and natural conception as an unlikely possibility. Whether I am able to have children or not, I know I will still be able to be a mother one day if I choose to be, so I am at peace.

Not long after this news, I got another diagnosis. To figure out why I was struggling to use my left leg and falling often, I saw specialists in Tennessee and Arkansas, some of whom I was on the waitlist to see for quite some time. Several nerve conduction studies revealed that I had permanent nerve damage. In all likelihood, this was the cause of my fall in the apartment when I was startled by Fancy and the cause of many other falls that followed it. I tried physical therapy and even dry needling, a process where specialists would stick thin needles into my leg and twist them around in an attempt to "wake up" the nerve, with no improvement. I am limited in both motion and sensation, and the radiation to my pelvis is most likely the culprit.

While my damaged nerves are not anticipated to heal or regenerate, I have gained strength in the muscles around those nerves and am able to do things that I never imagined I would be able to do again, such as lifting my leg while sitting, going on evening walks around the block, and even taking kickboxing classes. PaPaw remained the most positive with my leg and still encourages me to try and work past my limitations. He believes in me and continues to remind me how blessed I am.

When I shared the news of my nerve damage with my dear friend Maggie, she reassured me, saying, "It's okay if the nerves in your leg are dead, as long as you're not." Sometimes, I repeat this to myself to let it really sink in . . . *It's okay if the nerves in my leg are dead, as long as I'm not.*

To me, death is symbolic that one's work on earth is done. While my health indicated that death was near, I did not die. Transplant showed me how much I really am living on borrowed time. During a reflective conversation with Dr. Stine one day, he described a transplant as "a little science, a little art, and a little voodoo." This was such an accurate description of the balance transplant takes. All of my doctors are excellent, but this chapter of life would not have been possible without Dr. Frangoul's outstanding work. He was the link between me and my donor—all of it brought full circle as a gift from God.

This gift of life encouraged me to be direct and go after what I want. As I'd seen with too many friends already, life is short, perhaps much shorter than we anticipate.

52

Whenever I have scans, bone marrow biopsies, tests, or even lab work, I'm always prepared for something to be off. On the outside, I remain calm, but on the inside, I am on edge. When results look wrong, I try to quickly narrow down why. I usually know the reason, though, and it tends to not be the easy or preferred one.

At 18 months post-transplant, I had reached the milestone of only needing lab work monthly. I was thriving and finally felt like I had my life back. In June, my labs looked great, per usual at that point in my treatment.

But by July, I noticed a drop in my platelet count. My white blood cell count was not low, but lower in comparison to the stable count for months prior. I knew instantly. I could feel my voice shake as I tried to ask Dr. Stine why my counts were down without revealing my nervousness. He reassured me that it was likely just a fluctuation and that perhaps the summer cold I had just gotten over had played a part.

No, I thought to myself. *My platelets have dropped too much without a known cause.*

Dr. Stine reminded me that we have to see a downward trend in my counts before there is a need to do a test on my marrow. I nodded my head, but I knew. He kept his composure and not one thing about his physical response implied he thought anything was wrong, but we had been down this road together, and I knew that he knew.

Bre and I had made plans the month before for an impromptu sister trip to Chicago, and I didn't want to give it up. I confirmed with Dr. Stine that it was safe enough for me to fly on a plane with my decreased white blood cell count.

The following week, Bre and I boarded a plane to Chicago. Her then-boyfriend was stationed there, and Naina was living there while completing her oncology fellowship. Bre and I agreed it would be fun for the two of us to travel together, and we would both have someone to visit. We were ecstatic to explore a new city and felt so grown to be traveling without our parents. The trip was only a few days, but I planned a detailed itinerary with all of the attractions, restaurants, and stores. We went on a river cruise, peered over the 360 Chicago, and stuffed ourselves with deep-dish pizza. I was serious about the shopping and scheduled an entire day just for the Magnificent Mile.

The trip was refreshing, especially since I was anticipating the results that I already knew deep down.

When I returned home, I showed Mother the bruises

that covered my legs. She noticed they were not just on my legs though. My back, shoulders, arms, and abdomen were bruised, a clear giveaway that my platelet count was low. She assured me everything was okay. I quietly wondered if she was just oblivious. She later shared that she went to her bedroom and cried that night. She knew too.

The following week, I was due for labs. Since I was at home for summer break, my grandpa ordered my lab work. I went into my home hospital, calm on the outside. During the five-minute drive from my house to the hospital, I imagined how I would react when I saw my lab results. I wanted to remain calm and not cause a scene. I could go home and cry all I wanted to but not in the hospital wait room.

When the lab technician handed me the results, she informed me that my counts were all decreased and that my white count had been flagged as low. My platelets were 68, as opposed to a normal healthy 200–300, and my white count was 1.4, in contrast to a normal healthy 4.5–8.5.

Whenever a lab count is flagged as low, the lab tech is required to call the doctor who ordered the labs and inform them. My grandpa had ordered the labs, but the lab tech didn't want to call him. He was recovering from a triple bypass and aortic valve replacement surgery that had taken place only two weeks prior. She was concerned that the decreased lab work would send him into a panic, and she likely didn't even realize what I realized. I was relapsing.

I sat down on a chair in the waiting room and called

Mother, who was anxiously waiting at home. My voice was shaking, but I knew what had to be done, and I couldn't wait the five minutes it would take to drive to her.

She picked up on the first ring. "Hello?"

All I could choke out was, "They're down."

"What are? The numbers?"

I read them off. She was the warrior mother she always is. "Okay, you're okay. Just come home and stay strong."

I could hear the fear in her voice, and although I was anything but alright, I told her that I was alright and that I'd see her soon. I headed to my car.

When I walked in the house, Mother, Daddy, and PaPaw were gathered around the dining table.

"Alright," I said, sternly and confidently. "Who do we call?" I asked.

Mother nodded. "Tennessee."

I called and got the nurse's desk. I told a familiar nurse the situation and asked her to have one of the doctors or Misty call me back soon.

Next, I called Dr. Stine's nurse, Carol, at ACH. I informed her that I'd been in contact with Tennessee and was waiting on a response. Carol asked for the numbers, and I shared. I can't remember what she muttered back, but her voice was tighter. There was nothing she could do at that moment except wait. Without testing my bone marrow, there was no way to know for sure if I was relapsing, but my labs dropping and the mysterious bruises were strong signs. Carol having decades of experience and not being able to offer much reassurance was just another signal that this was something to worry about. Everything I had gained back suddenly felt so temporary.

When Tennessee called back, they wanted me to drive up immediately. The following day, Mother and Daddy drove me from Nashville to Nashville, yet again. The next morning, I had a bone marrow biopsy and the sample was sent to Seattle for further testing.

We waited to get home, and then we waited to hear the results. The game of cancer is one big waiting game. Waiting to get a phone call. Waiting to see a doctor. Waiting to hear a plan. Waiting to start chemo. Waiting to finish the plan. Waiting to get results. Waiting to relapse. Always waiting. Waiting is the toughest. Moments seem like days. Eventually, Dr. Domm called me with the results.

The leukemia was back.

Later that day, I received my third cancer diagnosis: relapsed Acute Myeloid Leukemia. I spoke with Dr. Stine on the phone. He was collaborating with my Tennessee team, as well as with some of the other pediatric oncologists at ACH.

By Monday afternoon, I had already had several phone conversations with my doctors and my parents regarding treatment. We all agreed that I needed to start chemo immediately and that I would eventually need a second transplant. I had maxed out on the type of chemo that was their first pick. My doctors carefully weighed my options. Dr. Stine warned me that if they went with their first line of treatment, my heart would be too weak to go into transplant. They needed to get rid of the leukemia without giving me something too toxic. We were walking a fine line, and every patient's body is different. How sturdy the line my body was offering wasn't clear though.

53

Dr. Stine warned me that I may become extremely sick, and he was wary of the damage that chemo had already done to my body. We decided to do another round of Mylotarg, the drug for which I originally went to Dr. Frangoul. When I first received it, it was not approved by the FDA, and my Arkansas hospital did not have access to it. By this point in my treatment, it had been approved, and I could receive it in Arkansas.

The day before I restarted the chemo, I went into clinic to review the plan. I also met with general surgery to consult having another central line placed. This would be my fifth central line or port, so there was not much that needed to be discussed. The appointment was a formality, but I went, and while I was there, listened to a resident who was fresh out of medical school attempt to explain to me what a central line is and how it works before I clued him in on my history.

After he left the room, I logged onto my school account.

When my previous diagnoses occurred, I was mid-semester and was able to work out a transition with my teachers and professors to complete my work online. I didn't have any official online class options for the courses I needed, and it didn't seem logistically possible to approach new professors and try to work out a plan since the semester hadn't even started yet. Hot tears filled my eyes as I hit submit to drop all of my classes for the upcoming fall semester.

Most of my familiar nurses looked at me with the saddest eyes, but I tried to not be sad. I didn't want anyone to be upset, so I tried to show them that I was okay. When I was walking out of my clinic room and passing the nurses' desk, I came across their daily huddle. Amy, the nursing director, saw me and excitedly hugged me, asking how I was doing. Apparently, she had no clue that I had relapsed. When I told her, her face dropped, and I could feel the sorrow in all of my nurses surrounding. Amy hugged me tightly and assured me that she would come say hi while I was staying on the floor.

That night, Mother and Daddy stayed with me in my apartment as I spent one last night there. I gathered items that I wanted to take with me to the hospital and my family would work on packing my apartment up within the following week. My nurse practitioner, Katherine, would write a letter to help me terminate my lease due to my health.

I was devastated to be leaving the apartment that represented how far I had come. I was just beginning to believe that cancer was behind me when, once again, it pulled everything out from under my feet.

The following morning, I had surgery to place my central line and was admitted to the floor. I began chemo again, and it was not long before challenges were presented.

First, I noticed a rash at the top of my thigh. Over the next few hours, it fanned out to completely cover my legs. The strangest thing to watch, it would rise and fall in an undulating pattern so that it appeared to be moving. It didn't itch but was warm to the touch.

Over several days, I constantly took photos on my phone to document the moving rash. Specialists came in to examine me. One night, it appeared so nasty that Mother had my nurse phone the oncologist on call. Dermatology came and examined it. The cause was never officially determined, but we believe that it was just an adverse reaction to the chemo. My doctors now joke that if a symptom is listed as a rare possibility for a drug, I will definitely present that symptom.

By the second dose of this round of Mylotarg, I began having respiratory problems. It felt like each breath was more shallow, and the time between breaths increased. It would have been easier to breathe with a stack of bricks on my chest. The pain in my lungs from lack of air deepened. It took too much effort to breathe, let alone speak. The drug was causing my blood pressure to drop extremely low and my heart rate to rise. This can be a sign of going septic, so my care team was constantly in and out of my room and closely watching my vitals. I struggled to make it the few feet from my hospital bed to the restroom. It would take Mother, Bre, and a couple of nurses assisting me and a chair in between so I could take a break.

The respiratory issues would finally begin to subside once it was time for the next dose of chemo, which led us to point fingers at the chemo as the cause. My team made the decision to double the infusion time and half the dose. As my nurses, Mother, and Bre stood over my bed watching, there seemed to be an improvement. The drug had been just a little too much for my system to handle.

Between medical obstacles, I enjoyed spending time with my team—my nurses especially. There were several new nurses on the unit that were only a year or two older than me, making it easy to form bonds. Ramon quickly became a favorite. We enjoy similar music, and he would always hang out in my room during his break so we could gossip. He would tell me all of the staff secrets, and I'd share the tidbits I knew as well. Mostly life-event stuff like who was getting married or having a baby, the gossip with him made the nurses relatable, and it was nice to discuss something other than cancer or chemo. While Ramon was fresh out of nursing school and new to the oncology world, he did a fabulous job at making my hospital stay easier.

The nurses weren't the only medical professionals I enjoyed spending time with. A team of doctors would round every morning, and by then I knew all of the attending oncology physicians well. The attendings rotated who was on call every week, and they were always accompanied by nurse practitioners, fellows, residents, and med students.

One morning, Dr. Stine was on call and in charge of rounds. The meeting with him and all of the younger doctors shadowing him was typical, until the end. As he was wrapping up the meeting, he turned to the medical students in the back and said, "If any of you are struggling to manage your time or need some organization tips, I would encourage you to visit with Kaden. She is the planner girl."

We all laughed. "It's true," I said, pulling a cart full of planners, notebooks, pens, and stickers close. "I have more at home, but this is what I brought for the hospital." They all *ooh*-ed and *ahh*-ed, but I didn't think much of it.

Late that afternoon, there was a knock at my hospital door. A blonde-haired girl entered wearing a large backpack and holding a clipboard in her hand. She looked to be not much older than me.

"Are you up for a visit?" she asked. I excitedly agreed, and she pulled a chair near my bed. "I'm Hunter. I'm in med school, and I was here during rounds this morning. I'd like to know more about your planners."

This really thrilled me. We talked for nearly an hour about planners. When it came time for her to leave, she promised to come back the next day. She kept that promise and visited me every day during her rotation and even continued once her rotation shifted to a different unit a couple of weeks later. We talked about planners, but we talked about other things as well, like our career goals and dating. She didn't treat me like an object to be studied, but like a friend. It especially meant a lot to me that she would take time out of her busy schedule of clinicals and studying to sit by my bedside and visit. Thanks to a joke from Dr. Stine about my love of planning, our friendship grew, and we are still in touch today.

The staff learned when I was in treatment in high school that I enjoy staying up late at night and sleeping late into the morning. A kind moment happened when the head of the oncology department, Dr. Becton, was on call one morning. When he reached my room at the end of the hall, he gently opened the door and peeked inside. I was sound asleep. According to some of the medical students who visited my room later, he closed the door, turned around, and announced to the team of medical professionals following behind that they would be taking a break from rounds because "the princess is sleeping."

The medical students who recounted this weren't much older than me and were at the very bottom of the chain, whereas Dr. Becton was at the top. They were in awe that he put everything on hold to let me keep resting. I wasn't surprised though, because my doctors spoiled me. While Dr. Stine was my primary oncologist in Arkansas, Dr. Becton was also very involved in my treatment, and I had grown close to both.

We remained in communication with my transplant team,
weighing donor options for a second transplant. I still had several perfect matches on the registry, but we were not quite sure
we wanted a perfect match this time. Choosing a match that
was not completely perfect can lead to developing some graft-
versus-host disease to fight off any potential leukemia cells. In
the past, we had not wanted graft-versus-host because it could
cause severe health problems like organ failure. Now, we were
wanting a little, so that my body, the host, would rile up my
graft cells and they would fight harder. Provoking the donor
cells in my body was a balance because we wanted them to fight
the leukemia hard, but not fight my body too hard.

Andrew was a strong donor candidate. He had tested as
a 7/10 match in comparison to Bre testing 5/10. When we discussed this plan, I was extremely hesitant. My concern was that
if Andrew were to donate and the transplant were to fail, he

would feel guilty. While there would be no fault on his shoulders, I would never want him to feel responsible or pressured. Eventually, we decided to reach out to a perfect match different from my first one.

For weeks on end, I was low on blood, causing me to be particularly irritable. Despite my sulking, PaPaw, Mother, and Daddy refused to acknowledge my grumpiness. PaPaw would be so kind when I felt bad, simply reminding me to be thankful.

When my counts recovered from chemo, it was time to test my marrow and see if the chemo had been as successful as we had hoped and prayed it would be. Misty called me a couple days after the procedure with the results: negative. I was unsure if she meant that there were not enough cells in my marrow to produce a good sample for testing. This had happened many times when testing after chemo. After all our time working together, she must have known my pause meant that questions were ping-ponging through my head. She quickly clarified, "No! I mean the test for leukemia is negative!"

The chemo had pushed me into remission.

"And, the new donor has agreed!" she shared, with a zing in her voice. I felt relieved to know we did not have to further explore the possibility of my brother being my donor. My team had reached out to a then 21-year-old male with a different blood type from me, and he agreed. He had not been on the registry when we were searching for a donor with my first transplant, so I was relieved that his motivation to join the registry and donate was fresh. It seemed incredible that a guy close in age to me wanted to do something so selfless. My generation often gets a bad rap for being selfish, yet this guy did not even know me and took personal risks for me. He was going out of his way to save the life of a stranger.

When we shared the news with Andrew and Bre, my brother's response was golden. He said, "Kaden's done this twice. The cancer must be tired, 'cause she's not tired. I know she will beat it quick." It was warming to hear his innocent faith in me. My parents always did a wonderful job of explaining to my younger siblings what was going on with my health and treatment, but when Andrew was younger, they wouldn't necessarily emphasize the urgency of my diagnoses. This shaped the outlook he has on my treatment even today. He understands the seriousness, but he believes in me, which gives me courage to continue moving forward.

A few weeks went by before I made a quick trip back to Tennessee on Halloween day. It was two weeks prior to my transplant date, and I had to have another bone marrow biopsy and some extra testing done for insurance purposes.

Two days later, I had made it back home and was sitting on the couch in my parents' living room when Dr. Frangoul called with the results. The bone marrow biopsy determined I was minimal residual disease (MRD) positive, which translates into a small amount of leukemia being seen in my biopsy results. This was not considered a relapse, but rather a "refraction." Essentially, the leukemia was not quite responding to the treatment like we wanted. Either the clear marrow results from the few weeks prior were not accurate or the leukemia had gone away and quickly returned.

We decided to do a small round of chemo to bridge me over to transplant. Dr. Frangoul was confident that the total body radiation that we were planning to do as part of my pre-transplant protocol would take care of the amount of leukemia present. While this was not great news, it was not the worst, because I still had options, and I was still a candidate for transplant.

We completed the bridge chemo, and I began packing for several months away in Tennessee. When it was time to leave home, I was emotionally drained, yet hopeful for one more shot at life. I looked out the window of Daddy's truck and wondered if this would be the last time I'd see home. I looked at the rocking chairs on the front porch and wondered if I'd ever sit there again during a storm. I knew I was heading into my own storm of life, and I had no choice but to walk through it.

55

When I returned to Tennessee, Dr. Frangoul met with my parents and me in clinic to discuss a few details, one of which was a living will. He advised me to document what my preferences were if I were to be placed on life support and warned me that a second transplant came with even greater risks. I opted for a power of attorney instead, because it felt too difficult to know what I would want with such a wide variety of ways that transplant could go wrong. I placed the power in my parents' hands and told them to decide based on Dr. Frangoul's confidence in any potential situation.

I privately instructed my parents, "You know one of the reasons I like him as my doctor is because he is willing to try things that other doctors might not. If he has a card up his sleeve and I can't make the decision, I want to use it. But if at any point he starts to show hesitation . . . that means that he has probably exhausted all options. Let that be the sign." They nodded understandingly.

Later that afternoon, I was admitted to Centennial and immediately prepped for surgery. My central line had been finicky and needed to be replaced.

The post-op experience was not pleasant. Daddy was in the waiting room, and they refused to bring him back until my pain was managed, but they were in no rush to manage it. The nurse took her time to call for the CRNA to bring pain meds. She also started an IV in my arm with no gloves. Through the grogginess, I confronted her and asked her if she was supposed to start an IV without gloves, to which her response was that she could if she was just giving a medicine. I knew this was wrong, but between the pain and post-op sedation, I was not able to continue the conversation.

While I was crying out in pain and waiting for meds, Leigh—a nurse practitioner who began working with my transplant team after my first transplant—came downstairs to check on me. She sat, held my hand, and tried to distract me with conversation. We discussed my plans for a big charcuterie board on my birthday in the coming month and likely other topics, but the memory is blurred. I had not known Leigh long, yet she had gone out of her way to comfort me post-surgery. It felt good to have someone like that on my side in Tennessee, especially in a moment when I was vulnerable and struggling to advocate for myself.

Twice a day for four consecutive days, I had total body radiation. I had fresh Steri-strips on my chest from surgery and the material on my skin increased the risk of a burn. I also was instructed by my doctors to go without a dressing over my central line, a concept that my home hospital did not support. I tried to go without a dressing, but after crying out of fear of germs infecting my line and sending me septic, my doctor agreed I could put a tiny piece of dressing over my line to make me more comfortable. There was no gauze or padding underneath though, making it painful over a fresh surgical site. Despite the pain, I was content with the compromise.

Total body radiation was physically challenging and not in any way I could have predicted. I was required to stand on a platform with clear plexiglass walls pressed against my body. I could not move during the radiation and a bicycle seat was placed on the platform as a fall precaution. One radiation oncologist, who was not my doctor but worked in the unit, was less than kind about the situation.

The dilemma was that it was difficult for me to stand over the seat *and* extremely uncomfortable to sit on the seat without moving for twenty-plus minutes. I found myself trying to hold my body weight with my arms to avoid the seat, but would eventually lose the strength to push off of my arms. It was impossible to hold my body weight up over the seat for more than a minute or two, let alone the nearly twenty minutes for each session before turning around and repeating the radiation.

As I was choking back tears, the radiation oncologist sternly told me, "You are just going to have to get over it. Everyone has to sit on the bike. It's the rule."

As I continued crying and attempting to do what he insisted, he harshly instructed, "Move your leg here. Step forward."

I tried, but because of the nerve damage, I couldn't move my leg. I begged, "Can you help me? I am having trouble moving it."

Louder this time, he robotically repeated, "Move your leg. Step here," as I pleaded to not use the bicycle seat.

One of the techs repeated my words, explaining, "She can't move her leg," because he wasn't listening. I dropped down from holding my body weight up with my arms and tried to adjust to a position that gave me the least amount of discomfort. It felt like all I could do was resign myself to the pain, count down, and move on.

When I was leaving radiation that day, some of the nurses in the radiology clinic asked me if I had any celebrity crushes. After the horrible experience with the radiation oncologist, it was nice to talk about something lighthearted.

I grinned and answered "Ian Somerhalder! I love Damon on *The Vampire Diaries*."

They all laughed and we discussed his role on the show.

I said, "I considered using my Make-A-Wish to meet him. I ended up choosing a European vacation and that was really cool . . . but that's how much I like Ian Somerhalder."

They all giggled and the conversation shifted, but I was glad to walk away on a more upbeat note.

When it was time for radiation the next day, I arrived

less than excited. It was physically challenging because my entire body was covered in burns, and I was mentally worn down by the idea of having to return. As the tech wheeled me in a wheelchair through the doorway of the radiation room, I noticed pictures of Ian Somerhalder were taped to the wall.

I began laughing and one of the nurses said, "We thought pictures of your celebrity crush might give you something to focus on while you're standing for the radiation."

We all continued laughing, and I thought to myself what a unique way this was to help a patient cheer up. It meant a lot that nurses who I didn't know well were trying to think of something that might make me happy, despite the difficulty of total body radiation and the conflict I had with the rude physician about the bike.

The radiation treatments only lasted four days, but they were long and difficult. Beyond the physical toll it took on me, burning my hands and face, it was emotionally draining. Constantly bartering with the doctor about what I was physically able to do took every bit of my energy.

56

When it came time for transplant, I was both eager and exhausted. The last transplant had initially been a success, but ultimately only lasted so long. Would the same thing happen again?

My friends from Dallas, David and Carol Basso who founded 1 Million 4 Anna, were in the city. During the transplant infusion, they stopped for a visit. Besides the scholarship and research support they've funded, they've also provided a great amount of emotional support for me, as well as other Ewing's kids and teens across the country.

Besides a bit of anxiety, the day of transplant was uneventful—exactly how I prefer it. Once again, the treatment and the transplant combination resulted in mucositis. My throat began shedding. As I lost the layers of lining within my throat, I could not help but think of how it resembled all that I have lost with my cancer diagnoses. I knew that with better health, the lining would heal and new cells would form, just as with time, I would heal from the damage that cancer had wreaked on my life for years. Before my body would begin producing new cells, I would be severely low on blood and especially low on platelets.

My nose bled for what seemed like days, constantly dripping. We began transfusing at least once a day, sometimes twice, in efforts to combat the bleeding. I have mastered handling many things with my health and treatment, but nose bleeds still make my stomach weak and my brain feel airy. Several days of constant nose bleeds were really beginning to take their toll on me.

On Thanksgiving, Mother and I watched the Macy's Thanksgiving Day Parade while my favorite transplant nurse, Eileen, started my platelet transfusion. Just a few minutes into the transfusion, something felt wrong. I couldn't quite tell or describe what it was, but I knew something felt off. My vitals looked great and all of my numbers were in normal ranges. Eileen and Mother reassured me that I was fine, but I persisted.

Then, it became difficult to breathe. There was this itch deep inside my throat that would not go away. My body felt heated and itchy all over. Eileen hooked a nasal cannula up to give me some oxygen and quickly pushed IV Benadryl into my line. It was difficult to keep my eyes open and hold my head up. I asked Eileen in a murmured slur if she had given me the Benadryl yet. She had. She would later joke with me that she had practically slammed my line and given me a large dose quickly.

During this time, Mother called Daddy and instructed him to hurry to the hospital. Andrew, Bre, and her then-boyfriend, who was visiting for the holidays, followed behind. Bre understood the severity of the situation without having all of the details. She instructed the boys to stay in the hall as she quickly followed Daddy into my hospital room. The respiratory therapist switched my nasal cannula for an oxygen mask.

Voices were clear and my thoughts were clear, but my body wouldn't do what my mind directed it to do. It seemed like a metaphor for my whole fight, my body never doing what I wanted it to do. And at this moment, it wouldn't move. I felt stuck. I struggled to keep my eyes open. I was very much aware and in the room, yet I was simultaneously drifting into my own world.

Mother kept trying to get me to sit up and look at the parade on TV. She was encouraging me to take a sip of Sprite, but I refused. I could hear my nurse call Dr. Frangoul and tell Mother that they were going to give me steroids. I heard new voices full of panic. From there, it was all black and faint sounds.

While my brain was slipping away, I tried to use the awareness I had left to silently pray out to God. I begged Him to save me.

As my vision cleared up and I felt more grounded with the world, I noticed how many people had crowded into the room and around my hospital bed. Some of the faces I recognized as my nurses and doctors, but most of the faces were unfamiliar. The number of people who had been working to save me made me realize how serious this episode had been. My breathing felt easier, though. I had made it.

57

My nose continued to bleed and my platelets were still severely low. Because we were transfusing daily, Dr. Frangoul proposed a platelet holiday to give my body a day of rest, especially in light of the reaction the previous day. Calling it a platelet holiday felt like making a celebration out of nothing, but I was ready to create some real fun on my own.

It was Black Friday, and I was looking for a way to organize the sticker sheets that I use to decorate my planner. I ordered twelve letter size, pink glitter pouches and had them sent to the apartment. The following week, Mother brought my mail to my hospital room. We were both equally surprised to see so many pink pouches. While I had been looking for a new organizational tool, this was not it, and I did not even recall ordering so many. My nurses and I had a laugh, as online shopping sprees were becoming fairly common for me when heavily medicated. I have been known to shop online both as Kativan and when fresh out of sedation, but it was always an exciting surprise when an unexpected package arrived. I viewed it as a surprise gift from myself to myself.

The daily platelet transfusions would continue until I was discharged 22 days post-transplant. It took me 23 days to leave the hospital after my first transplant, so I joked that I'd been more efficient with the second.

Once I left the hospital and shifted to staying at the apartment and going to clinic daily, I began to experience extreme fatigue. I slept through most of the days and woke only when it was time to go to clinic. I stopped eating and was less than willing to share with my transplant team how sluggish my appetite had become. I had to force myself to sip on water and eat a bite or two every day. Eventually, my appetite picked up, but it would take nearly a year for it to completely recover.

It was not long before I reached the 30-days-post-transplant mark. After the first transplant, I was quickly able to reach 0% leukemia in my marrow and 100% donor cells. While that is the best possible result, the main goal was no leukemia revealed in an MRD (minimal residual disease) test and at least 97% donor cells at the 30-days-post-transplant mark.

On my 21st birthday, we anxiously awaited the results. I slept most of the day to combat my intruding thoughts of my body failing to accept the cells. Mother and Bre had kept themselves busy by making two large charcuterie boards to celebrate my birthday. That evening, while eating dinner, I received an email from Misty. She wished me happy birthday and informed me that my marrow was 100% donor. My body had successfully taken to my donor cells. We were ecstatic.

While I did not spend my 21st birthday out partying or doing anything I would have expected, and we were still waiting on my MRD test that would determine if there were any leukemia cells in my marrow, hearing the best possible news on the first part of the results was a great gift. I spent the rest of the night with my family watching the *Overboard* movie remake on our apartment couch.

The following morning, Daddy and I went into clinic. As we were getting ready to leave, the MRD results arrived from Seattle via fax. Leigh had been in the room with me and had gone to check. When she returned with Dr. Domm instead of by herself, I knew the results were not what we had hoped for.

The two sat down and informed me that my bone marrow signified .1 percent leukemia. While this was less than my pre-transplant numbers and still only a tiny amount, the ultimate goal was for there to be absolutely no leukemia.

We decided to stop my immunosuppressant medication, tacro, early. Typically, we would have waited until at least 100 days post-transplant to stop it, but we needed to try and induce some graft-versus-host disease.

As challenging as it was to hear that the results still showed leukemia, it was even worse to share the news with Mother. When Daddy and I walked into the apartment, she was sitting on the couch. I couldn't even get seated next to her before tears streamed down my face. I didn't have to say many words for her to know that the leukemia was still present. She wrapped her arms around me and squeezed me tight.

Daddy and I relayed the few details of the new plan. My marrow would be tested again in thirty days. My doctors were researching treatment options. This was a turning point, as the treatment plan that we had put so much hope into had not worked. The problem with options is that the more you use, the fewer you have.

The days to come were full of hope and coziness. Once again, we had six people and three dogs staying in a two-bedroom apartment over Christmas. The space was tight, but it was nice to be together, especially considering the circumstances.

When it came time for my 60-day marrow test, Daddy prayed over the marrow sample before it was sent to Seattle.

Two days later, I was lying in bed at the apartment, nearly asleep. Dr. Domm called with the results: MRD positive .01%. There was still leukemia, but even less. They decided to start me on another chemo regimen, Decitabine. I had taken this drug once before, and it had been easy. It dropped my counts some but did not have any nasty side effects. We also made plans to start Donor Lymphocyte Infusions (DLIs), infusions of baby T cells from my donor—essentially a transplant boost. The goal of this was similar to stopping my immunosuppressant medication early: to induce graft-versus-host disease.

It was just a few days before I started my 25th round of

chemotherapy. This would be my first round of chemo outpatient in a clinic rather than inpatient in the hospital. I would go every day for five days and repeat every four weeks, depending on whether my bloodwork recovered.

One afternoon, Keagan's mother, Robin, left a voicemail message asking me to call her back. I could hear the pain in her voice. I had known Keagan stopped treatment and wasn't doing well. I instantly began crying and didn't want to call her back because I knew what she was going to say. After a few minutes, I pulled it together and returned her call. My fear was correct.

After spending nearly his entire life fighting brain and spine cancer and having dozens of brain surgeries, Keagan left this earthly world and went to be with our Heavenly Father. I had no words and knew there were none to make it okay. I wanted to hug her tight, but I was over 500 miles away.

When I saw Keagan in Arkansas before leaving for transplant, I knew it was unlikely I would see him here on earth again. He had stopped treatment because he was out of options and did not have much time left. Before some really bad days when the cancer began to take over his little body, he had some good days without the treatment to make him sick and weak.

The shock hit hard. It still breaks my heart to think of all that he went through and how hard he fought, only to die. I selfishly wish that Keagan was still here, but I believe that he is complete and healed in Heaven. Keagan's death was yet another reminder of why I fight: in honor and memory of all of my friends who have fought and won, advancing beyond this earthly life.

Sometimes it is easy for me to get frustrated with how long I have been in treatment. Sometimes I get frustrated that the cancer keeps returning. I know that the negative thoughts are always there on the sidelines, waiting to consume me if I let them. But then, I think of Keagan. I think of Keagan and the promise we made to each other to continue fighting and beat childhood cancer. Keagan held up his end of the deal by fighting until his very last day. He never gave up, and while cancer took so much from him, it never took his strength or perseverance. He won because he kept his spirit. I owe the same to Keagan, at the very least. We promised each other to keep fighting, and I intend to never stop. On the days I can't do it for myself, or for any other reason, I do it for Keagan.

When I reached the 100-days-post-transplant mark, we checked my marrow once again. I went home to Arkansas and received a call two days later with the results: MRD negative! Once again, the leukemia was gone. We will never know for sure if it was the extra chemo or if the donor cells kicked in, but either way, the last few leukemia cells were eliminated.

We decided to continue doing the chemo for at least 18 months. My team also began the process of reaching out to my donor to ask him to donate lymphocytes—a type of white blood cells that are an important part of the immune system—for DLIs. This new treatment was uncharted territory because I didn't know any other patients who had done it. I was desperate when I returned to Tennessee for another transplant, and that desperation had only deepened when it wasn't working. I was hopeful that DLIs just might be the boost that my new transplant needed to be successful.

I would be able to do the chemo outpatient at my Arkansas hospital. While over two hours away from home, it was still much more convenient than doing chemo in Tennessee, eight hours away.

In late spring, we learned that the donor had agreed to donate the lymphocytes. I traveled to Tennessee once again and received my infusion. The first dose of cells all fit in one syringe. The first dose was the easiest because it was fresh and did not have any preservatives mixed in. The other doses would have preservatives and would be a bit larger. I would feel extremely heated and have trouble breathing easily while receiving the cells, but the reactions would stop each time as soon as the infusions were over.

One thing that had gotten me through the months surrounding my second transplant was the hope of attending my annual planners' conference in Vegas that May. I knew I'd be cutting it close, if I could attend at all. The conference admins had graciously reached out and offered for me to attend as a guest, free of cost. Mother, Daddy, and Bre planned to travel with me. Two weeks ahead of time, it was looking good, so we booked our flights. I had to research hospitals near the conference hotel and make an action plan with my transplant team in preparation for a potential fever while traveling. My doctor wrote me a note for airport security explaining the central line surgically inserted into my chest and the medications in my carry-on, and I rented a scooter to be able to get around the hotel and the city easily.

On the day of travel, Mother, Daddy, and I drove to the airport with plans for Bre to join us the following day after her final exams. Our first flight was significantly delayed. Usually, we are able to request for an airport employee to push me between gates. When we arrived in Dallas for our connecting flight, there was nobody waiting with a wheelchair like we had requested. We were crunched for time to make our connecting flight. We noticed a vacant airport wheelchair nearby, so I plopped into the chair with my suitcase in my lap, and Daddy began pushing me.

We followed closely behind Mother, but neither of us knew exactly where we were going or the directions to our gate. When Mother took the escalator and we took the elevator, she got a little ahead of us. Mother stepped onto the sky train and we were close but not quite there. I excitedly told Daddy to move faster so we could catch the sky train. As we approached the doors, Daddy's speed increased. I felt the wheels catch on the gap between the train and the platform and the suitcase in my lap flew onto the train. The wheelchair caught, but the momentum kept me going, and I landed on the floor. It hurt, but I was more concerned about missing our flight. Over my shoulder, I hollered, "Hurry, Daddy! Come on!" He stepped on just as the doors closed and the sky train sped off. Everyone surrounding us looked on in horror as I burst out laughing. While I had an immune system equivalent to a newborn being thrown onto the nasty sky train floor, it was so absurd there was nothing to do but laugh and get back into the wheelchair.

At the conference, I was able to see many of my friends in the planner community who had supported me for five-plus years, including Naina, who has been by my side throughout much of my treatment. I left feeling refreshed.

By the time Pandora and I returned to college, I'd completed 28 rounds of chemo, two stem cell transplants, and 40 doses of radiation.

Until the Covid-19 Pandemic, I continued chemo and DLIs while remaining a full-time student. The risks of catching Covid while receiving chemo outweighed the risks of stopping chemo, so I kept on through my 35th round.

Some days it felt hindering not to be as far along in college as my friends or to have to stop and go to the hospital for tests, labs, and chemo. On those days, I tried to focus on the positive. When I was looking, I discovered I could find good in the smallest and most unexpected ways: a good parking spot at Chick-fil-A, a new episode of a favorite TV show, online shopping for a cute purse, or painting my nails a different shade of pink. Finding small things to be thankful for made the hard days a little easier.

The farther I move from the time in my life when sickness was all I knew, the easier it is to fall into the trap of frustration when things don't work out the way I want them to. Even knowing this is a trap, I still fall prey to it. I suppose it is human nature to get caught up in things that don't matter.

Yet, as Mother has often reminded me, "It's never as bad as it seems." This advice helps ground me. Some days are harder than others, but her words remind me to keep moving forward. I learned what it is like to struggle and suffer at a young age, which placed life in perspective. My journey has been made bearable thanks to good people: my family, my friends, my doctors and nurses, my community. I've remained wrapped in support, and all I've had to do was fight.

Fighting has been the easy part. It was instilled in me long before cancer. From kindergarten to senior year, my classmates and I were taught how to be Scrappers. We were taught an intense competitive spirit that led to winning. We ate orange sugar cookies, "Scrapper cookies," in the cafeteria every game day. We were told that we bled orange, and we believed it. We wore Scrapper jeans as little girls and again as seniors. We were winners not because of luck but because we were fighters.

Before I was a Scrapper, I was just Kaden. Google the name Kaden, and you will see that it has Celtic origins, that it means "fighter." Some might say that both the name Kaden translating to "fighter" and the mascot's spirit being instilled within me from such a young age are merely ironic or have happened simply by chance. I believe it's more. I think God shaped me to have a fierce nature—giving me a personality that some have thought and will continue to think is too much, a gritty spirit which has helped me push through. I can't help but believe that He who formed my personality was behind all that prepared me, right down to my identity as Kaden and as a Scrapper.

Then again, in the peds cancer world, everybody fights. Not fighting is not an option. Even when it is, it isn't. Seeing so many cancer kids fight and die is by far one of the hardest parts of my life to witness and explain. Perhaps the real winners are the ones who give it everything they have.

60

Three years post-transplant, weeks before graduating college, and one month before I turned 24, my college friends and I squeezed around a table at my favorite Little Rock restaurant, Heights Taco & Tamale. We were celebrating three years of my life, made possible by a successful transplant. Our table was covered with platters of tacos, and we indulged in salsas, guacamoles, and cheese dips. Around the table sat friends I had met in the previous three years as well as a lifelong friend, Brooke, who cheered with me in high school and who had been among the first to see me the night Maddi shaved my head. We treated it as a birthday, because for me, transplant was a new chance at life.

Toward the end of the meal, I proposed a toast to my donor. I had learned a few months before that his name is Christian. He is my age and lives in Germany. After two and a half years, we both had the opportunity to request information identifying each other through the international registry. While we have not had the opportunity to meet in person due to distance, we have been able to communicate via social media and text messages. He is always humble about his act of kindness, but I see it for no less than what it is. He saved my life.

I shared with my friends that because of him, I was able to sit at that very table with them. He provided me the opportunity to live and to celebrate my life in big and small ways. I'm not quite sure if that fully resonates with friends that entered my life later, but part of me enjoys that. Some of my friends grew teary-eyed, but each of them grinned as we all lifted our glasses and cheered, "To Christian!"

As I have returned to life beyond the hospital, cancer fades as the entirety of who I am and increasingly becomes one aspect of who I am. Yet, I am able to recognize that everything I have done and will do post-transplant would not be possible without Christian and my first donor, who remains anonymous. The identity that I am growing into as I navigate my mid-20s is possible due to my donors' generosity. I once only dreamed of the life I have now, a life of normalcy and opportunity. It seemed like it had been both a short time and a lifetime ago that I was praying for a miracle.

My joy at the simple fact of being able to look confidently toward the future was inexplicable, and I felt that joy beam through my body as I looked at my friends and grinned. After parting ways with my friends that evening, I shifted to thinking about what the next three years might look like.

They include starting law school, which will itself take another three years. While so many things prepared me for my fight against cancer, I believe that my fight against cancer prepared me to be an attorney. Being sick for so long forced me to learn how to learn how to advocate for myself, and now I am ready to advocate for others. Our shared experiences of my fight also inspired Bre to become a nurse who steadfastly supports her patients.

That desire has also taken the form of a nonprofit organization that Bre, Andrew, and I founded. The Unseen Faithful (TUF's) mission is to support siblings of childhood cancer patients. We noticed during treatment that many siblings are often unseen, yet faithful—just as Bre and Andrew were throughout my treatment. TUF sends cards and gifts, which we call Happy Mail, to siblings across the nation. Bre and Andrew pick out the Happy Mail and make cards, Mother is in charge of mailing the packages, and I handle the fundraising and business side. As I work to raise funds, I am afforded the opportunity to advocate for a specific group that I believe plays a huge role in fighting pediatric cancer.

Some people say I do too much. Many suggest that I slow down or take it easy, but that has never been my thing. The fight never really ends when you have to fight as hard as I did. Fight. Fight.

Fight. This is what all cancer kids do. If I try to come up with another word, there simply isn't one. If cancer is so much waiting, it is also so much fighting. Fighting, fighting, over and over again. It feels impossible to separate myself from it.

As Asher's mom Susan once said, "We didn't go through all of this just to twiddle our thumbs." I couldn't agree more. Shifting from fighting at this level to twiddling just wouldn't feel right. Maybe if I wasn't trying to do big things, it wouldn't feel like I was fully honoring my friends who didn't get to keep living their lives.

When I look up, I see *Asher*'s big spirit and spunky soul. I think of IV pole decorations and nail polish during blood transfusions. Rainbows remind me of her soft giggles.

I see *Taylor* strumming the air guitar and playing with sock puppets. He was so matter of fact. His wittiness is left with me. Whenever Aerosmith plays on the radio, I'm reminded of Taylor.

I even think of the kids and teens that I never knew with lives and families not so different from my own. Teens like *Anna*, who fought Ewing's years before me. Her death inspired her family to found 1 Million 4 Anna and brought me Kyla and Lauren.

I see *Kyla*'s gentleness and how she always thought of others. Her last words to me were, "I'm in a lot of pain, but still fighting hard. How are you?" How kind it was of her to ask how I felt as she was on her deathbed and to still dream of planning a trip to visit. She was the epitome of grace.

I think of **Lauren** persisting through college despite relapse and inspiring me to chase an education and write about my challenges with the fight. She reached out when I was diagnosed with leukemia, saying, "I believe we can both get through this." She died two months later. Her tenacity was strong, and her outlook remained positive.

I see *Scout*, a girl who fought Ewing's when I fought Ewing's and leukemia when I fought leukemia. My childhood preacher was her preacher at the time of my first diagnosis, and he reached out to encourage me to keep an eye out for her. Our paths crossed during treatments, and I often wondered why our stories were so similar, yet ended so differently. She had a Boston Terrier like my mom's and liked *Lilo & Stitch* like my sister. When I learned she died, I sat alone in an infusion room and cried.

I think of **Kenzie**, a fellow makeup-lover, when I apply my own makeup in the mornings. She was just a couple of years younger than me, and we bonded over makeup trends during endless hours in the hospital.

I think of baby **Oakley**, who grew up in Southwest Arkansas like me and also had to travel out of state in search of a cure. His body grew from toddler to young boy but would stop growing forever at just five years old. He liked Army men and race cars.

I am reminded of **Lilly**, Oakley's best friend. She too fought Ewing's Sarcoma and was often seen by Oakley's side in the hospital. They died within months of each other, but their friendship lives forever.

I remember **Josh**, the boy who played basketball. He was the first kid I saw hooked up to a pain pump. We often took turns being on the upside of the battle. The last time I saw him, he came to visit me in the hospital when I was hooked up to a pain pump for the first time. He was doing better then, and I had such strong hope that he would be able to keep playing ball.

I am reminded of **Jarren**, who played baseball. I think of him when I watch a baseball game, just as I think of Josh when I watch basketball. Both of these boys were healthy, active teens before cancer.

I think of **Riley**, a girl I met through Keagan. She had been fighting brain cancer for years. She always seemed to be smiling or laughing, an inspiration to all.

I think of **Elijah**, who had been fighting for over ten years when I first met him. He was a few years younger than me. His mother, Dawn, recognized me in the halls of 4K and invited me to meet Elijah in his room. He sat on his hospital bed playing the guitar, and when I asked him if he participated in the Beads of Courage program, he laughed and quipped, "I have buckets of beads, too many to try to string."

With both of their own kids admitted to 4K, Dawn and Robin had come to sit with me while I awaited results the night I learned I had leukemia.

Robin asked, "Is no news good news?"

When I slowly shook my head and struggled to find the words, Dawn quietly whispered, "Sometimes radio silence is a bad thing."

I nodded and knew they knew. Keagan had been fighting for a long time and Elijah even longer. They'd been through all of this before.

Keagan died right after my second transplant, and Elijah died later that year.

I am often and especially reminded of **Keagan**'s precious character. He loved Batman and grilled cheese sandwiches. He came to visit me in the hospital before I left for my last transplant, and I knew it would likely be my last time to see him. His laugh was contagious, and he seemed so healthy, so happy. It still makes no sense why he felt so good that day, and I felt so sick, yet I made it and he didn't. Orange sunsets remind me of the promise we made to each other, to fight for the rest of our lives.

Life is far from easy post-cancer, but I am inspired and grateful to have known so many determined friends who fought the good fight. Whatever happens next, I feel them with me every day. Driven by their strength, I will continue to find my own, knowing that I'm never alone.

Pandora and Kaden's Graduation and Law School Announcement

KADEN PEEBLES

Kaden Peebles is a Juris Doctor candidate at Oklahoma City University School of Law where she is class president, a Hatton Sumners Scholar, and a member of Phi Alpha Delta. A magna cum laude graduate of the University of Central Arkansas, she was selected as the History Department 2021–2022 Student of the Year.

An avid volunteer, Kaden loves serving the hospital closest to her heart and prominently featured in *One True Scrapper*, Arkansas Children's Hospital. Since 2015, she has served as an ACH Patient Ambassador, representing teen and young adult patients of Arkansas. Since 2016, she has been a member of ACH Circle of Friends, planning events and raising funds for the hospital, and has served on the ACH Youth Advisory Council, leading the implementation of patient Wi-Fi and handicap-accessible doors (as described in *One True Scrapper*). Kaden was chosen as the 2018 Arkansas Children's Hospital Foundation Rookie of the Year. Since 2016, she has represented the Make-A-Wish Foundation as a Make-A-Wish Ambassador.

Kaden has received numerous awards for her volunteerism and community activism, including being selected as the 2018–1019 Nashville Arkansas Chamber of Commerce Community Hero and receiving the 2015 True Scrapper Award. Kaden has also represented foster children in Faulkner County, Arkansas, as a Court Appointed Special Advocate (CASA) since 2021.

Kaden is Co-Founder and President of The Unseen Faithful, a nonprofit for pediatric oncology patient siblings whose mission is to recognize and spark joy for siblings through monthly "Happy Mail."

To learn more about how you can get involved or to nominate a sibling, visit theunseenfaithful.com.

Join in Kaden's Insta inspo
@kadennn5 and @thedailykaden_

CPSIA information can be obtained
at www.ICGtesting.com
Printed in the USA
JSHW020738210623
43508JS00003B/10